'Duncan writes in such a way [hungry to seek the face of Jesus
the presence of God through e
evokes your emotions, his use
alive and you come away stirred, with a longing to live
deeply.'
Anne Calver, Unleashed Church

'The shallows of a swimming pool are usually busier than the
deep end. I suspect many don't like feeling vulnerable when
the water begins to overwhelm them – but Duncan has
consistently resisted the comfort of the shallows. I've seen
him time and time again look out over the vastness of the
ocean and make decisions to discover deeper waters. In this
wonderful book he shares his motivation and key principles
learnt in his adventures of the deep. I'm sure you will also be
inspired and empowered to go deeper.'
Mark Pugh, Lead Pastor, Rediscover Church, Exeter

'*Live Deeply* is developed through many years of effective
Christian practice and faithful stewardship of the gospel of
Jesus. This book is very inspiring, professionally researched
and thought-provoking, particularly in this post-global-
pandemic season. It will spark a deep desire to draw close to
God and make you hunger for His presence. It will encourage
a good personal devotional life by creating intentional
moments of stillness in God's presence to allow the Holy
Spirit to speak to you. Leading a presence-led life will
champion spiritual fulfilment and foster a process of
maturity in you as a disciple of Jesus.

'*Live Deeply* is an incredible resource for all who seek to
maximise opportunities for effective ministry in not just
living a Christlike life, but also in sharing and modelling

God's character in showing love, kindness and compassion as disciples of Jesus.'

'As fellow church leaders, working in unity in the same city, it has been our joy for many years to see the fruit of Duncan's life-giving approach to ministry first hand.

'We love his authentic faith, humble posture, generous spirit and evident passion for God's presence. The keys he shares in *Live Deeply* will shape us profoundly and lead us into rhythms that will keep us deeply rooted in Jesus, who is Life! Thank you, Duncan, for letting us benefit from your rich inner world.'

'*Live Deeply* acts as a mirror for the reader; while reading it, you will see yourself in the stories told by Duncan about his life's journey. The book challenges the status quo and encourages deep soul searching.

'*Live Deeply* encourages its readers to be real about their spiritual state and to crave for God's presence, using Jesus to measure where they are rather than comparing themselves with others.

'This book does not just identify the need for God's presence but also teaches principles that help us to experience and dwell in His presence. I strongly recommend it to anyone who is desirous of becoming a finished product of God and chooses to live deeply. By our fruit, we shall be known.'

'Duncan and I are so different in many ways – perhaps that is why we get along so well. He is an author and I don't read books. When Duncan sent me the manuscript, I started reading it because of our friendship. I finished reading it because he has something to say that is worth hearing.

'He would describe me as an "activistic" person – I could easily slip over into being a workaholic. Perhaps that is why his introductory comments about people who go through life skimming the surface caught my attention. High-energy people who move fast through life/work/ministry, covering a lot of ground, moving from one opportunity to the next and enjoying the "buzz". Duncan is not that person; he has intentionally "dug deep" – you cannot build as he has built, faithfully over decades, by skimming. He puts it so well when he says we need to celebrate both the fruits and the roots.

'Book lovers will love this – the rest of us need it more than we realise.'

David West, Bethel Sozo UK

LIVE DEEPLY

It's time to get out of the shallows

Duncan Clark

instant
apostle

First published in Great Britain in 2024

Instant Apostle
104A The Drive
Rickmansworth
Herts
WD3 4DU

British Library Cataloguing-in-Publication Data

A catalogue record for this book is available from the British Library.

This book and all other Instant Apostle books are available from Instant Apostle:

Website: www.instantapostle.com

Email: info@instantapostle.com

ISBN 978-1-912726-79-0

Printed in Great Britain.

Stay with what you heard from the beginning, the original message. Let it sink into your life. If what you heard from the beginning lives deeply in you, you will *live deeply* in both Son and Father. This is exactly what Christ promised: eternal life, real life!

I've written to warn you about those who are trying to deceive you. But they're no match for what is embedded deeply within you – Christ's anointing, no less! You don't need any of their so-called teaching. Christ's anointing teaches you the truth on everything you need to know about yourself and him, uncontaminated by a single lie. *Live deeply* in what you were taught.

And now, children, stay with Christ. *Live deeply* in Christ. Then we'll be ready for him when he appears, ready to receive him with open arms, with no cause for red-faced guilt or lame excuses when he arrives.

(1 John 2:24-28, *The Message*, my emphasis)

Contents

Foreword

Our destiny is not a certainty but a God-given opportunity, and our choices are important in determining our final legacy! What do you want your end game to be? What are the intentional choices you need to make to get there? I remember God challenging me to move into a deeper level of trust concerning my finances. I would have considered myself a generous person as I was always willing to support people in need. But when God asked me to give beyond my budget, that was a new level. By giving this more substantial gift, it meant I no longer had enough money to pay all my incoming bills over the next weeks. I was stretching into new levels of trust with God. I was no longer in control of my money! I had always wanted to leave a legacy of generosity... now I was learning how to actually do it.

In this book, *Live Deeply*, Duncan not only shares the revelation of living a life that will satisfy you completely, but he also unpacks the strategic choices you need to make to move your life from a good place to an outstanding position. None of us would actively choose to live in the shallows of our potential, missing the mark of all God has for us. But many of us do miss this mark by not being intentional enough in all the little decisions of everyday life. We need to learn the secrets of waiting time with God, knowing these waiting times are *never* wasted times. God has plans that are dependent on our obedience, so that we arrive at the right place, at the right time, in the right frame of mind, with the right experience… ready to do all He has called us to do. There are no shortcuts. We need to learn this grace of waiting, prayer and surrender to Him.

This is a season where God is challenging us to dig deep and then stretch wide. Many of us are carrying fresh vision for the next phase of our lives. The temptation is to run with all these various ideas and plans and spread ourselves thin with endless activity. The result is that we have no reflective or conversation time with God, and we end up feeling empty and distant in all our relationships. We want to be productive – but before we can produce abundant fruit, we need to be rightly rooted. No fruit without good roots!

As Gordon and I have connected with Duncan and the Coventry church, we have always loved the way they are hungry to activate what they hear from God in practical expression. I remember when we were working in Africa with Reinhard Bonnke, and we were sensing it was time to explore working in Malawi. As we asked for instructions and programmes, Reinhard turned towards Gordon and said, 'Just listen and *do* what the Holy Spirit tells you to do! Now go!' As we move into new landscapes and opportunities, we first need to listen. We cannot work with just 'good' ideas – we need those God-inspired ideas that we receive directly from heaven. We need to have a rhythm of life where we download, outwork the instructions and then reload!

While walking by a river recently, I was fascinated watching one of the birds. It would paddle along in the shallows, seemingly just going in circles, then suddenly it would flip upside down and disappear. Later, I would spot it some distance away, swimming lazily again. Then I smiled to myself: I realised that everytime this bird dived, it was getting food. In the deeps of the river it knew how to find sustenance and then it was ready to come back to the surface of the water and explore further. The best food in God's river of life is in the deeps. We, like this duck, need to learn to dive into the depths, trusting God, and find the rich food for our souls.

> Now to the God who can do so many *awe-inspiring things, immeasurable things,* things greater than we ever could ask or imagine through the power at work in us …
> (Ephesians 3:20, VOICE)

God has plans for us. He has plans to surprise us with more than we can measure or imagine! You have a Father who is ready to give you more. He loves you and knows your weaknesses and still has an upgrade for you! As we choose to live in the deeps, we will discover that He has *kept the best for us until now.*

Rachel Hickson with Gordon Hickson
Heartcry for Change, Oxford, UK
September 2023

Introduction

I've changed.

I'm not the person I once was.

In my twenties I was primarily focused on my purpose. My goal was to discover why God had given me the gifts, skills, personality and opportunities I had been given. I wanted to ensure that I lived from a sense of calling, that I was clear about my assignment and that I was moving forward with a clear sense of purpose.

In my thirties my focus began to shift. I started to concentrate on my performance. I wanted to be the very best leader I possibly could be. I wanted to be better than those around me. I became consumed with numbers and statistics. Those numbers and statistics informed my identity; how I felt about myself.

In my forties something changed. I began to focus on presence. God's presence. My primary goal became the creation of a way of life and an approach to leadership, where the pursuit of the presence of God became my 'one thing'. I started to create healthy rhythms where I would arrange my life around practices and activities that fostered a deeper intimacy with God. To be clear, I still had a definite sense of purpose and a God-given assignment. I still worked hard and wanted to maximise the gifts and opportunities I had been given. But there became a less-than-subtle change in how I tried to live and lead.

Performance-driven leadership has its benefits. It gets the job done. The organisation advances. It elevates the leader into the limelight. The leader gets the applause. It creates energy, momentum and movement.

But there's a dark side too.

When I was solely performance-driven, I found my mood going up and down depending on the stats. I found my drive for excellence easily tipped over into perfectionism, and I became easily irritated when my performance (or the performance of others) wasn't faultless. I found that I would be drawn into comparison and competition with other leaders, other churches and other organisations. I would get the job done, but my heart suffered.

Learning to live a presence-led life has changed me. It's changed how I lead. I'm learning to stay in my lane and love the assignment I've been given, rather than comparing my calling to the guy or girl who has greater influence than me. I'm learning how to lead from a posture that is devoid of fear, panic and striving. I'm learning to be the non-anxious presence in the room. I'm learning to live from a foundation of gratitude and thanksgiving, rather than complaint and grumbling.

I'm learning to live deeply.

In Luke 6:40, Jesus taught that His followers go through a process of growth until they are 'fully trained'. He hinted that there are stages of discipleship where a person moves from 'starting out' to 'partially trained' to 'fully mature'. We should not be surprised that we don't arrive at full maturity overnight. In fact, that goal may never be completely realised. But as the years pass, and as we become increasingly surrendered to the Father's will, we engage in a slow process of becoming more like His Son, Jesus. It takes time.

That's been my story. After a couple of decades of pursuing lesser goals, I set my heart on something of greater value. I had become increasingly concerned about the incongruity of trying to lead people into the depths while I was paddling around in the shallows. I could hear the invitation of the Father to go deeper. I started to find ways to order my life around what matters most. I tried to figure out how to live a life that was in line with my deepest desires. I began to learn what it looks like to live deeply.

I wrote this book at the commencement of my fifties. I am a long way from being 'fully trained', but I have also taken a few steps toward maturity. Although I am a leader, and from time to time I will write from a leader's perspective, I am primarily a follower. I am a disciple. And so this book is written for followers. It is written as an invitation to those who want to know God deeply and serve Him fully, with hearts that have been shaped by His presence. It is written for those who long for something more.

This book wasn't written just to be read. It was written to be reflected upon and even discussed. Some readers may choose to pull out their journal after each chapter, reflect on the content and then scribble down their thoughts. Others may prefer to read the book with a small group of friends and then discuss their observations, share the ideas in the book that create resonance or resistance in their hearts, and then pray for each other. Whether you're reflecting or discussing, I've added a short prayer and some questions at the end of each chapter that are designed to be a springboard from which you can dive into deep waters!

What is offered here is not a comprehensive vision of the deeper life; it is my simple observations and experiences of what it takes to step out of the shallows and into deeper waters. I pray you'll sense the smile of your heavenly Father over you and that your heart will be 'strangely warmed'[1] as you hear His invitation into a new way of living.

---

[1] As John Wesley found. See www.ccel.org/ccel/wesley/journal.vi.ii.xv i.html (accessed 31st August 2023).

Live Deeply

As I write these words, our world is still feeling the effects of the many challenges that a global pandemic brought. Of course, COVID-19 had a profound impact upon almost all spheres of our society. Education, healthcare, social care, financial markets, hospitality, retail and many other sectors failed to escape the reach of the pandemic.

Since I spend a large proportion of my life in church-world, I have found myself having multiple conversations about the effects of the pandemic on local churches and on the faith of those who follow Christ. There were many predictions that people would leave the Faith, leave the Church and leave orthodox Christian teaching. As I listened to those projections, I started to wonder what would be the defining characteristics of resilient Christians. Those who would remain faithful and fruitful in the aftermath of the pandemic.

I should be clear about what I mean when I use the word 'resilient'. Before the pandemic I would picture a resilient person as being a bit like a brick wall. Immoveable, unshakeable, they just stand firm. In recent times I've changed the analogy. I've started to see the resilient person as being like a tree that can be blown around in a storm but, because of its deep roots, it can bounce back to its original shape and position once the strong winds have passed. I've started to ask myself what followers of Jesus can do that will increase their levels of resilience in a time of great pressure and upheaval.

At the point of asking those questions, I found myself reading the New Testament letter of 1 John in my personal devotions. It was written at a time in history when people were also leaving the Faith, leaving the Church and being tempted to abandon sound doctrine. The apostle John takes the opportunity to write to those early believers and teach them how to live a resilient life.

I find Eugene Peterson's rendering of these verses so helpful:

> Stay with what you heard from the beginning, the original message. Let it sink into your life. If what you heard from the beginning lives deeply in you, you will *live deeply* in both Son and Father. This is exactly what Christ promised: eternal life, real life!
> … *Live deeply* in what you were taught.
> And now, children, stay with Christ. *Live deeply* in Christ.
> (1 John 2:24-28, *The Message*, my emphasis)

John writes to a fledgling church, to new believers who are under significant pressure to walk away and quit the Faith. His advice is both profound and embarrassingly simple: 'Live deeply.'

Their resilience in the storm was dependent on each of them *living deeply*.

Now, let me be honest with you. I have an uncomfortable relationship with that word 'deep'. First, because almost every pastor I know has been criticised by members of their congregation because their preaching isn't deep enough. Even the greatest preachers throughout history would testify to congregants approaching them to ask for 'deeper teaching'. I've been there too.

I have also arrived at a conclusion that when people ask for deep teaching, they really want to hear something they don't understand so that, after the sermon is finished, they can turn to the person they came to church with and say, 'I didn't understand a word of that. It was so deep!'

For me, the request for deep teaching has become an occupational hazard, and when someone thanks me for preaching a simple message that everyone can understand, I secretly think to myself, 'Oh no! I'm not deep enough!'

And second, I feel uncomfortable with the word 'deep' because I know that one of my greatest temptations in my walk with the Lord can be summed up by two words that are the opposite of deep: shallow and skimming.

I have found that it is possible to live such a full and busy life with so many distractions that my spiritual life, and specifically my devotional life, can become dangerously shallow and I end up skimming the surface of what should be a deep relationship with God.

As I reflect on my childhood, I have many fond memories of visiting British seaside locations for summer family holidays. Annually, my dad would help me scour the beach for the flattest stones and would then teach me to throw them at maximum speed so that the flat surface of the stone would skim along the surface of the sea, and we would then count how many times it would bounce before it disappeared from sight.

It's a perfect picture of one of my greatest temptations.

And I don't think it's just me.

Our lives become so full of activity, with so many digital distractions, that we end up reading our Bibles like we're scrolling social media, we end up praying like we're creating a soundbite, and we end up building a surface-level relationship with our Father in a rush. It means that the words 'shallow' and 'skimming' accurately define our connection with God.

And yet, John tells us that if we are to live a resilient life, we must *live deeply*.

So what did John actually mean when he wrote, 'live deeply'? Well, if we look at the same text in a different version of the Bible, it may help us:

> I am writing these things to you about those who are trying to lead you astray. As for you, the anointing you received from him remains in you, and you do not need anyone to teach you. But as his anointing teaches you about all things and as that anointing is real, not counterfeit – just as it has taught you, *remain in him*.
>
> And now, dear children, *continue in him*, so that when he appears we may be confident and unashamed before him at his coming.
>
> (1 John 2:26-28, NIVUK, my emphasis)

For John, living deeply requires us to prioritise these two things. Remain in Christ. Continue in Christ.

To *remain* in Christ describes an intentional lifestyle where we rearrange our lives to deepen our connection with Him. It's all about staying close to Jesus.

To *continue* in Christ describes a desire for our character and our conduct to be shaped by His presence in our lives. It's all about becoming more like Jesus.

That's what it means to live deeply.

And before we go any further, I should be crystal clear: *deep* is not the same as *serious*. *Deep* does not equal *boring*. *Deep* does not equate to legalistic, sombre, pessimistic or solemn. People who are living deeply are usually joyful, content, creative and at peace. Deep people love to celebrate and sing. In fact, they are often found with a smile on their faces because they have a relationship with the happiest Being in the universe!

Deep people have learned to 'remain' and 'continue' in Him.

And that's what the focus of this book will be. Later we'll be unpacking what it means to 'continue in him' by examining four heart postures that are required of us if we are to live deeply in this world with the character of Christ. But first, we'll dig into what it means to 'remain in him' and how that can produce a deep life.

Of course, when John instructed those under-pressure believers to 'remain in him', he was only repeating a command that he had heard from Jesus; an instruction he recorded in his Gospel:

> Remain in me, as I also remain in you. No branch can bear fruit by itself; it must remain in the vine. Neither can you bear fruit unless you remain in me. (John 15:4)

It's a strange-sounding directive, isn't it? It may be helpful to offer alternative wording that helps reveal the original meaning:

> Stay joined to me (John 15:4, ERV)
> Live in me (John 15:4, GW)
> Make your home in me (John 15:4, *The Message*)

Or even:

> ... connected to Me (John 15:4, VOICE)

Each translation suggests that our spiritual depth and vitality is wholly dependent upon us recalibrating our lives so that we have a life-giving attachment to Jesus.

More than a decade ago now, my wife Helen and I trained as foster carers with our local city council, eventually becoming adoptive parents. During that process we were taught about 'attachment theory' and the importance of a child having a secure base from which they then live their lives with confidence. My basic understanding of the theory is that from an early age, a child needs to develop strong emotional connections with significant caregivers (usually their parents), so that they grow up knowing that they are loved, safe, secure and valued. It is from that *attachment* they can love others, build healthy relationships, act with courage and take appropriate risks. It is the *attachment* that enables a child to live a well-rounded life.

I believe that what happens in the physical is often mirrored in the spiritual. If we are going to live full and abundant lives (John 10:10), it will require an intentional attachment to Christ. And the obvious question is, 'How do I do that? How do I strengthen my connection to Jesus so that I move away from a lifestyle of skimming and into living deeply?'

Well, in the following chapters I'll share with you some practical suggestions that I hope will answer those questions, but before I do, let me paint you a picture of what that intentional intimacy looks like.

In fact, it's not my picture (and it's not even Leonardo da Vinci's!), it's John's. In chapter 13 of his Gospel, John paints the picture of the Last Supper. Jesus is talking to His disciples about what is to come. He talks about His betrayal and His sacrifice. It's incredibly upsetting and confusing for those who have given up everything to follow Him. There is a storm that's about to blow through their lives.

Where is John at that moment?

He is 'leaning back against Jesus' (John 13:25).

At a time of great upheaval, John is leaning back on Jesus' chest. He can hear His heartbeat. He feels the warmth of Jesus' body next to his. He is looking out into the world from the perspective of his closeness to Christ.

I believe that this is an almost perfect picture of what 'remaining in him' looks like. It's a wonderful depiction of living deeply. Leaning back on Jesus, so that the peace in our hearts matches the peace in His heart.

We are not leaning back on our news reports.

We are not leaning back on our social media feeds.

We are not leaning back on the opinions of critics.

We are not even leaning back on the things in our lives that are good but are also prone to unexpected change.

We are leaning back against Jesus.

And here's something I find quite remarkable. While John leans back on Jesus, Jesus is leaning back against His Father.

Here's what John writes at the start of his Gospel:

> No one has ever seen God. But the unique One, who is himself God, is *near to the Father's heart*. He has revealed God to us.
> (John 1:18, NLT, my emphasis)

Similar sentiments that are used to describe John leaning back against Jesus are also used to describe Jesus leaning back against His Father's chest. It appears that John was as close to Jesus as Jesus was close to the Father.

And if that is true, the implications for us are huge.

John was just as human as we are, and yet he experienced a close connection to Jesus that enabled him to live deeply. I believe we can do the same.

I hear some of you saying, 'That's OK for John. He knew Jesus in the flesh. He could actually, physically, lean against Jesus. I can't do that.'

Well, I am going to suggest you can! In fact, I've designed the chapters that follow to show you how. I've written them as an invitation to ordinary people like me and you to step out of the shallows and into the depths. An invitation to create a lifestyle of intentional intimacy with Christ. An invitation to prioritise life-producing rhythms that bring us closer to Jesus.

And so, before we turn the page, let's determine to:
Lean back.
Remain in Him.
And live deeply.

Heavenly Father, I hear Your invitation to leave the shallows and step into the deep water. I am dissatisfied with skimming. I need something more. Take me deeper. I want to make my home in You. Amen.

For reflection/discussion

- What is your understanding of resilience? What are the defining characteristics of a resilient person?

- What is your current understanding of spiritual 'depth'?

- In what ways do the words 'shallow' and 'skimming' resonate with you when you assess your current relationship with God? Or do they create a resistance within you? Why/why not?

- Using your own words, how would you describe remaining in Christ and continuing in Christ?

SECTION ONE

REMAINING

Staying close to Jesus

1

Strategic Sitting

It was one of those emails that I could quite easily have missed. Just like you, my inbox is often littered with messages that don't even deserve to be opened. Offers to improve the condition of my body, my hairline and my bank balance without any effort on my part. A six-pack without sit-ups. Opportunities to make life-changing financial investments, where all I need to do is send my bank details and there'll be a large credit deposited very soon. You know the kinds of emails that I'm referring to. I suggest you don't respond to them!

And then, because I'm a local church pastor, I also receive occasional emails from God. Well, that's how they are sometimes worded. I'm informed by concerned church attendees that the drums are too loud, the lights are too bright, the sermon is too superficial or the coffee is too weak. And then, to give extra weight to their opinion, some authors conclude their communication with, 'Thus saith the Lord,' or something very similar that adds divine approval to their message. Well, this email could have easily slipped into that category.

We were right in the middle of the first coronavirus lockdown and, like so many other leaders, I was stumbling my way through a brand-new landscape, trying to make wise decisions that would help keep our church community connected, on mission, cared for and loved. There were some days I didn't want to make another pivot. I was wrestling with decision fatigue. And here was an email, purporting to be a message from God, with an instruction that would help me navigate the demands of this challenging season.

The unsolicited email came from a retired church minister, now in his mid-eighties. A gentleman I didn't know at the time. He had read a magazine article that I had written and, apparently, he had sensed an inner prompting from the Lord to send me a verse from the Bible that he believed would assist me. It was a short and simple verse, but it made a profound impact on me.

The verse is buried in the middle of 2 Samuel 7; a verse that takes us right into the middle of David's royal reign when life is going very well for him. It is a moment when it feels like everything David touches turns to gold. The Philistines have been subdued. Goliath is dead. Saul is dead. And because God has been good to David, he naturally wants to do something good for God in return.

David decides to build God a sanctuary. He wants to build God a home. After all the years of desert wandering, David wants to honour God with a permanent place to live; a grand temple that would reflect God's glory. So, with great enthusiasm, David shares his plans with his prophet and pastor friend, Nathan. Nathan gives the king permission to move forward: 'Whatever you have in mind, go ahead and do it, for the LORD is with you' (2 Samuel 7:3).

Nathan endorses David's proposal wholeheartedly, but also unthinkingly, because that night God speaks to Nathan and lets him know that He has other ideas. It turns out that God has no desire for David to build Him a home; in fact, it is obvious to God that David's grand plans to do something for Him would only serve as a distraction from what God wants to do for David.

The next morning, Nathan returns to the king and he withdraws the building permit. He pours cold water on the fire of David's enthusiasm. He tells him that the building project is cancelled because God has an alternative plan. A plan to build David a *house* instead.

At this point in the story, we arrive at the verse of Scripture that was lovingly presented as a word from God to me. It will probably appear as an insignificant verse. A trivial verse. And yet it is a verse that provided me with a tool that enabled me to live deeply and lead wholeheartedly through the pandemic: 'Then King David went in and sat before the LORD' (2 Samuel 7:18).

David sat.

This may have been the single most important thing that David ever did. Arguably more important than killing Goliath, honouring Saul and bringing the ark to Jerusalem.

David sat.

David was at his peak. He was in his prime. He was successful and powerful. But he was also godly. In fact, he loved God so much that he was bursting with expansive plans to do something great for God. Stopping David's momentum at this point was like trying to stop a runaway train. But David let himself be stopped by God. David went into the Lord's presence and sat down. He did not take a seat to negotiate with God. David sat in surrender. He surrendered his own plans and submitted to God's plans. Even though David was the king, he abdicated his royal authority to the King who is the beginning, centre and end of all things.

David 'sat before the LORD'. He just sat there!

In the dark days of the pandemic, this one verse offered me a means by which I could avoid being sucked into the black hole of leadership anxiety and fear. It presented me with a tool where I learned to trust in God's goodness, create space for encounters with His presence and receive His peace. I learned to sit before the Lord.

I've come to the conclusion that to live deeply, I need to embrace a lifestyle of sitting down. It's the kind of lifestyle I want to invite you to adopt too.

But because this invitation could easily be misunderstood, I need to explain what this invitation is not. It is not an invitation to laziness and inactivity. It's not an invitation to sit and scroll through social media. It's not even an invitation for introverts to get some 'me time'.

I like to call this practice 'strategic sitting', and instead of endorsing indifference, you might say that it's where the real action takes place.

I'm describing a lifestyle of intentionally sitting before the Lord. You open your heart to His loving presence. You listen for His voice. You ask Him to fill your soul with His power and His presence. You receive the affection of His heart towards you, and you turn the affection of your heart towards Him. You take a seat and invite Him to do a deep work in you. You surrender your desires, your plans and your great ideas to Him. You ask Him to lead. You are being strategic, not lethargic.

And while that may sound incredibly easy, I'm guessing that, in reality, many of us will find that incredibly hard to practise. So many of us are activistic, and we're secretly afraid that we might be caught out doing too little for God. We resist anything that feels like a pause button; anything that feels like being idle.

In my early days of local church leadership, I learned an inadequate, but very common, metric for assessing ministry success. It was described as the ABC of attendance, buildings and cash. I learned that if the church was growing numerically, had a good-looking building and enough cash in reserves to cover three months' expenditure, I was doing just fine. And then I discovered that my American friends added a fourth: butts, buildings, bucks and buzz!

Buzz?

That feeling you get when the room is crammed full of people and they sing their hearts out to God with passionate voices. That feeling you get when you finally lock the doors of the church after preaching your heart out to hungry disciples, knowing that you gave your very best. That feeling you get when you sit in the same room as the team you love and you strategise and plan for kingdom advancement, and at the end of the meeting you place your hands on each other's shoulders and you pray a blessing over each other's lives and homes. For a local church pastor like me, that's the leadership buzz.

And it's addictive.

Leaders or not, it's common for activistic people to live off this kind adrenaline rush and avoid the stillness that's found by sitting in the Lord's presence, simply because they are afraid of what they will discover if they do it.

In the stillness, we discover our unhealthy attachments, our mixed motives and our injurious idols. In the stillness, our deepest desires and our darkest thoughts rise to the surface. In the stillness, we ask, 'Who am I when I leave the crowds behind?' As we sit before the Lord, we start to wonder if we've been trying to gain the whole world while forfeiting our souls (Mark 8:36). In the stillness, we start to wonder if we've been drowning out our heart's persistent voice with our addiction to activity, progress and purpose. In the stillness, we wonder if we've been pursuing the wrong thing; we wonder if we've confused the pursuit of God with the pursuit of the *buzz*.

We avoid sitting in stillness before the Lord because we're afraid of what we might discover in our hearts if we take the time to do that.

At the time of writing this chapter, I have just returned from a five-day retreat at a beautiful centre in South Wales. It was a perfect opportunity to practise what I'm preaching to you. There was no internet connection. Very little conversation. Minimal distractions. I had five days set aside to sit before the Lord. A luxury, I know!

It took at least twenty-four hours for the leadership adrenaline to leave my body. I found it nearly impossible to resist the urge to compulsively check my smartphone. In my mind, I kept instinctively creating to-do lists, even when there was nothing much to do. It felt like going 'cold turkey' when, on the Sunday, I left a bustling, exuberant church community, where I am known by many, and then on the Monday arrived in the stillness of the Welsh countryside, where I am known by no one.

Eventually, the inner chaos started to settle. At first, I felt lazy and unproductive. I felt like I was wasting these precious days. I craved the feeling that comes when I achieve something. But then my soul settled. As the inner noise in my head and my heart abated, I found that I could hear God's voice more clearly. As my body took a break from incessant movement, I found that I became increasingly sensitive to the Lord's presence around me and in me.

I entered this retreat asking God what His invitations to me might be as I approached a new season of life. I found myself asking the Lord about my middle years, with twenty-five years of experience behind me and with twenty-plus years of adventure ahead of me. What were His plans for my life, for my family and for the local church I have the joy of leading? As I sat before the Lord, I learned that the answer to these important issues are 'heard' and not 'figured out'. These are issues of listening, rather than issues of the mind. I discovered that when I sit before the Lord, His Spirit witnesses with my spirit and, if I listen carefully, He communicates His plans deep into my heart, rather than relying on my ability to compute them cognitively.

It took some time, but as the days passed, I found my heart softening and my soul being restored. As I sat before the Lord, the stillness that surrounded me found its way inside me. The solitude and silence created an inner condition within from which I could better recognise and respond to His voice and hear His plans.

There are many reasons why we might avoid sitting in stillness before the Lord, not least the danger that He might redirect our good ideas and good intentions. But it's become my belief that when we avoid the practice of 'strategic sitting', we miss out on one of the most life-giving, heart-filling experiences available to us. I've attended many conferences and events over the years, hungry to receive vision, information and strategy, but I've come to believe that the most strategic thing I can do with my life is to intentionally sit in the Lord's presence each day.

For the first decade of my life as a leader, I arrogantly thought that I could live and lead from a heart that relied on occasional and spontaneous moments with the Lord. These days it's different. I practise 'strategic sitting' almost every day because I *need to* and because I *want to*.

I *need to* spend time in His presence because that's where I feel in touch with my authentic self. That's where I hear His words of love sung over me. That's where I see more clearly and more calmly.

I *want to* sit before the Lord, not out of duty, but from a deep desire to be with Him. I want to sit in the presence of the One who knows me completely. I want to hear the voice of the One who can lead me into life.

The reality is, very few of us will ever live in religious institutions where we can spend multiple hours each day in prayer without unending distractions. For many of us, the pressure of time and the demands of responsibility relegate 'strategic sitting' to a possibility rather than a priority. But I've found that the weight of work life and family life are more easily carried when I've sat before the Lord and surrendered them to Him each day, even if it's just a small portion of my day.

When David penned the words of Psalm 131, I wonder if he had his experience of 2 Samuel 7 in mind? He creatively paints a picture of what it looks like to sit in the Lord's presence:

> My heart is not proud, LORD,
> my eyes are not haughty;
> I do not concern myself with great matters
> or things too wonderful for me.
> But I have calmed and quietened myself,
> I am like a weaned child with its mother;
> like a weaned child I am content.
> (Psalm 131:1-2)

David reveals to us that there were many things in his life that were too difficult to understand and too weighty to carry. Many issues that were so complicated that they remained a mystery to him. But rather than trying to find an answer to every conundrum, he chose to calm and quieten himself before the Lord and be still in His presence. That would be enough.

David explains that instead of being like a nursing child who simply desires to be with its mother because of the milk it will receive, he has chosen to be like a 'weaned child' who can now get its food from other sources but chooses to be close to its mother only for the sake of closeness. For the sake of intimacy. Nothing else.

It's a beautiful image, and one on which we'll conclude this chapter. It doesn't have to be complicated. It just takes intention.

Choose a period of time (ten minutes will be just fine!).
Put away your distractions.
Find a chair.
Sit before the Lord.

Calm and quieten your heart.
Open your hands in surrender.
Become aware of His presence.
Embrace the stillness.
Listen for His voice.
Ask Him to fill your soul so that it overflows.
It's simple, but this is where the deep life starts.

Heavenly Father, I know that You love to meet me in the stillness. I also know that I'm often too distracted to meet with You. Have mercy on me. Help me to quieten my soul and my scattered senses, so that I can truly be with You, to be in Your presence and to sit at Your feet. Amen.

For reflection/discussion

- Put yourself in the shoes of David in 2 Samuel 7. How do you think you would have felt, knowing that your building project had been cancelled? What would you have expected God to say? What would you have said in return?

- Describe the places where you go to meet with God. What makes them such 'thin places' where God's presence can be felt and His voice heard?

- What makes practising solitude, stillness and silence difficult for you? What do you think the benefits would be if you were to practise these three things more often?

- Meditate on Psalm 131. How do you see the difference between a nursing child and a weaned child? What does that teach you about remaining in Christ?

2

Roots

As I've grown a little older and, more specifically, as my children have grown a little older, I have developed a love for my garden. For many years my lawn was the location for football matches, wrestling matches and Nerf wars. At some points in the year, there wasn't a single blade of grass to be seen. It became a dust bowl. Any plant that attempted to thrive was always threatened by imminent death, usually from an out-of-control football, out-of-control toddler or out-of-control teenager. But those days are behind me now and I love to take care of my garden. In my mind, I'm aiming for a lawn that looks like Lord's Cricket Ground and plants that are fit for the Chelsea Flower Show. Of course, that will never happen, but it's good to have a goal!

Gardening has taught me an important principle. Patience. I've had to learn that in order to produce beautiful blooms in the spring and the summer, a bit of patience is required. In fact, I've had to learn that most of the hard work that produces the flowers happens below the surface and deep in the soil. I've learned the importance of selecting the right location for each plant to be planted, so that its roots can do their two roles of creating an anchor for the plant, as well as absorbing the water and nutrients from the soil.

And here's the key observation from my life as a very amateur gardener: *everyone applauds the fruits, while no one applauds the roots*. Everyone celebrates the flowers, but no one celebrates what happens below the surface to produce them. No one gives away the roots, but many of us love to give away the choicest blooms. No one cheers for the soil. No one gets excited about the roots. No one instigates a standing ovation for what's happening, unseen, below the surface of the ground.

I think you get the point.

No one applauds the roots, but they are vital for the production of the fruits.

As is often the case, what happens in the physical is mirrored in the spiritual. The fruitfulness that God desires for our lives, and which is often highly visible, is very much dependent on our unseen roots.

If you are a follower of Jesus Christ, you have been chosen and appointed to 'bear fruit' (John 15:16), and that fruitfulness suggests that you are so fully connected to Jesus that you think like He thinks, you speak like He speaks and you act like He acts. Fruitfulness means that when someone tastes your life, you taste like Jesus (I know that sounds a bit weird, but it's the best I could do!). It means that you are so closely attached to Him that your life will produce visible results that make people say, 'Now, that's what it means to be Christlike!' You are living a fruitful life when people see 'love, joy, peace, forbearance, kindness, goodness, faithfulness, gentleness and self-control' (Galatians 5:22-23) flowing from your life. That's what a fruitful life looks like. In fact, that's what *living deeply* looks like!

And it's worth adding that Jesus has no plan for you to produce just a little bit of fruit. Just a small harvest. No! He has big plans for your life. He desires that you produce 'much fruit' (John 15:5). This is not a moderate, conservative plan. It's an abundant plan for your life. And He's not expecting your life to produce temporary results, but for you to have a long-lasting impact – to produce 'fruit that will last' (John 15:16). To be clear, God's mandate for your life is abundant, enduring fruitfulness.

The danger for many of us, in our rush to produce 'much fruit', is that we end up giving little attention to putting down deep roots. In our impatience, we forget the vital purposes of those roots, *anchoring* and *absorbing,* and we foolishly expect to be fruitful without paying attention to them. As this chapter develops, I would like to suggest three areas of our lives where we can be highly intentional about cultivating deep roots that will, in turn, produce great fruits!

1. Rooted in the secret place

You and I need a secret life with God. In most areas of life, secrets are unhealthy and often destructive. Hidden lives often cause great harm. Living a transparent life where you have nothing to hide is a virtuous goal. But I believe that it is healthy to have a secret life with God. Times of prayer where you talk with Him honestly, in a way that you wouldn't talk with anyone else. Moments of stillness where He speaks into your soul and you don't post His words on social media, share them with a friend or, in my case, turn them into a sermon illustration. You hide His words in your heart (Psalm 119:11). Your life becomes rooted in the secret place with Him.

The Gospels tell us that 'Jesus often withdrew to lonely places and prayed' (Luke 5:16). He then taught his followers to do the same:

> But when you pray, go into your room, close the door and pray to your Father, who is unseen. Then your Father, who sees what is done in secret, will reward you.
> (Matthew 6:6)

In Jesus' day, personal privacy was a difficult thing to source. Many families would live in one-room homes. They would eat and sleep together in that one space. Jesus knew that finding a private place for prayer would take some creativity. He hoped that His followers would find a store cupboard, an inner room, a cubbyhole from where they could pray in secret.

After leaving school at eighteen, my first proper job was working for a large UK bank. I was given a job title that sounded much grander than the role I actually played. I was called an 'advances assistant', but in reality I was in charge of photocopying, sending the post on time and making senior members of staff their morning coffee and afternoon tea. High pressure! Despite my lowly role, I was given one wonderful privilege. I was entrusted with the key to the stationery cupboard, which was more like a room than a cupboard, and I was responsible for keeping it well stocked.

In my late teens, my Christian faith came alive, and I was always looking for opportunities to read my Bible and pray. The stationery cupboard became my secret place. I would sneak my tiny Bible, with its minuscule font, into my jacket pocket, and I would turn fifteen-minute trips to check on stock levels into a few minutes of secret prayer.

As you read this chapter, I'm guessing that you might be trying to figure out how you can find the time and space to lay these roots of secret place prayer, especially if you are trying to juggle a variety of work and family pressures. Would you allow me to say a few things about that?

Being rooted in the secret place will require you to give God a portion of the best part of your day

I appreciate that we are all living different lives, we are in different seasons of life and we carry unique responsibilities and pressures. Therefore, there is no 'one size fits all' solution. There's no cookie-cutter approach to creating a secret place lifestyle. One strategy I do think is helpful, however, is to identify the best portion of your day, and then go into your secret place and spend some of it with God.

Some of you are early risers and you are at your best first thing in the morning. Some of you are late nighters and you come alive any time after 11pm. Some of you will be looking after small children and your home feels like a war zone, but there's one hour when everyone in the house is asleep. Some of you care for ageing parents, and the demands on your time seem endless, but each day there's a small gap when you feel like you can take a quick breather. Some of you will get a lunch break at work. Some of you will arrive at the office half an hour before anyone else.

So, despite our vastly different life circumstances, I would imagine that the majority of us have a 'best part of the day' where there are minimal distractions, and it's in those moments that we go into our secret place, we turn the affection of our hearts towards God and we intentionally spend time with Him.

Being rooted in the secret place will cost you

Let's be honest: pursuing this kind of lifestyle and putting down these kinds of roots will cost you. It will cost you time – time when you could be doing other important things. It will cost you sleep – sleep you could have had last thing at night or first thing in the morning. It will cost you productivity – opportunities to work more and get more done. Whichever way you choose to apply this teaching, it will undoubtedly cost you something.

I've discovered that so much of what God gives to me is free, but fruitfulness is always costly. I've learned that if I am going to invest in a 'history' with the Lord that no one else knows about, there's going to be a significant cost attached to that.

Being rooted in the secret place will require humility

Jesus makes many outrageous statements. This is one of them: 'apart from me you can do nothing' (John 15:5). Nothing!

One of the great challenges of being a follower of Jesus is that pride and fruitfulness tend to grow in the same soil. The great fruit that is produced from living close to Christ is often accompanied by the weeds of self-sufficiency and pride. Unless they are carefully monitored, even removed, the weeds tend to grow at a faster rate than the fruits.

The prideful, arrogant person believes that they can live their life in their own strength. They believe their personal and spiritual growth is an entitlement. They are happy to take the risk of spontaneous spirituality, and so they cease prioritising the secret place. They stop being intentional about 'remaining' with Jesus. Their life becomes a project in human striving.

The humble person takes a different approach. They know that if they detach from Jesus, their life will produce little or no fruit. They know that their only option is to go to their secret place, get on their knees and express their dependency on Him. The humble person acknowledges the negative dynamics of their independence and so they actively move towards daily encounters with the presence of God in secret. This way of life becomes their roots and, in turn, produces abundant fruit.

2. Rooted in His words

While we are digging into Jesus' teaching in John 15, it's worth picking up on His command that our lives are to be rooted in His words. It seems that the visible fruit we desire is produced when we allow His words to dwell deeply in us.

> If you remain in me and *my words remain in you*, ask whatever you wish, and it will be done for you. This is to my Father's glory, that you bear much fruit, showing yourselves to be my disciples.
> (John 15:7-8, my emphasis)

The original Greek word for 'words' in this text is *rhema*[2] which, according to Thayer's Greek Lexicon, means, 'that which is or has been uttered by the living voice'.[3] The 'words' of Jesus include, therefore, what He *has said* and what He *is saying*. You might put it this way: the 'words' of Jesus include what He *has* spoken through the Scriptures and what He *is* speaking today.

What He *has* said

First, I am describing those moments when you sense God speaking to you when you read the Bible. He speaks to you about how to deal with your finances, how to look after your family and how to work with wisdom. His written Word communicates to you the truth about your identity, your purpose and your mission. These words are a vital contributor to your fruitfulness, and that's why it's important that they are rooted in your heart.

In the first few weeks of joining the staff of the church I now lead, the previous senior pastor issued me with a challenge. He gave me a pack of small cards, on each of which was printed a Bible verse. There were around fifty of these cards and he challenged me to memorise them. Since I was (and am!) compliant and obedient, I got to work and committed each of these verses to memory. I walked around the local park, speaking them out loud. I positioned the cards in places where I would see them throughout the day. I recalled them, rehearsed them and remembered them as I was driving. Little by little I hid

---

[2] www.reflectingtheologian.com/logos-and-rhema (accessed 20th July 2023).

[3] www.bibletools.org/index.cfm/fuseaction/Lexicon.show/ID/G4487/rhema.htm (accessed 4 September 2023).

them deep in my heart, and now, twenty-five years later, I can still recollect almost all of them, and so when I need to know what God might be saying to me on a subject, I have a word from Scripture that's been rooted in my heart.

What He *is* saying

Second, I'm describing those moments when Jesus, by His Spirit, whispers some 'extra details' that are relevant for that precise moment. It might be the name of a specific person we need to forgive, a place we are to live or a job we should apply for. These 'extra details' will never contradict the general teaching of the Bible, but they will speak into the 'now'.

I've often reflected on the importance of listening for a 'now' word when reading the story of Abraham and Isaac. Abraham is told by God to take his only son and sacrifice him on Mount Moriah (Genesis 22:2). Though God's command seems illogical, Abraham obeys. He binds Isaac, places him on the altar and raises the knife to kill his son. At that moment God speaks His word a second time and tells Abraham to stop (Genesis 22:12). I've often wondered what would have happened if Abraham wasn't listening for the 'now' word from God. I guess he would have killed his son, believing that God would raise him from the dead, and thus the story would have been radically changed!

We need the words of Jesus rooted deeply in our hearts. We take delight in them. We meditate daily on them. We pray them over our lives. We allow them to shape the way we talk. We expect them to come to pass. As His words remain in us, hidden below the surface of our lives, they will produce much fruit; a visible demonstration that we belong to Christ.

3. Rooted in community

One final observation from Jesus' teaching in John 15. There is one vine and many branches. Obvious, I know! It's a simple reminder that the pursuit of this deep and fruitful life is not performed in isolation, but by being rooted in community. Of course, there is only one vine: Jesus. But there are many, many branches: people like you and me. I've figured out that I have a better chance of living deeply if I have other people walking alongside me who have the same goal.

> I am the vine; you are the branches.
> (John 15:5)

During one of the final COVID-19 lockdowns, I experienced something that I hadn't really experienced before. I experienced a brief bout of loneliness. For quite a few weeks I had been working in my office with very little in-person, face-to-face contact with other people, and I noticed something in my heart that I hadn't noticed before. I was lonely. By personality type, I am an introvert, so I am usually quite comfortable with my own company. But this felt different. I missed being with people. I missed my community.

Rather than feeling sorry for myself, I got to work and sought out and made contact with three people I knew could help me. A good friend, a mentor and a spiritual director.[4] I was honest with them. I explained that I had been feeling unusually lonely and that I needed some good people to talk to. They obliged. They loved me and it wasn't long before my heart felt full again.

I had learned a valuable lesson. To live deeply, I needed to have deep roots in community. My fruitfulness wasn't just dependent on who was *in me* (Jesus!), but also on those who were *around me*.

Let me suggest four types of relationship that I believe we all need:

Rooted in the company of a *tribe*

It's vital that you plant your life in a community that is larger than just you and your small group of friends. A community that believes in the same things as you (such as that Jesus is Lord – Romans 10:9), wants the same things as you (such as, 'on earth as it is in heaven' – Matthew 6:10) and generally thinks like you (such as with a renewed mind – Romans 12:2). We usually call this 'church'. While there is a consumer mindset epidemic in the contemporary Western Church that results in church-hopping and church-shopping, I believe it is very difficult to produce much fruit if you keep digging up your roots and transferring them to another pot every few months. You need to be rooted in a tribe.

Rooted in the company of *cheerleaders*

We would do well to intentionally find some positive, faith-filled people and deliberately spend time with them.

---

[4] A spiritual director is trained in the art of listening with another person to the Spirit's voice as they share their reflections on their life and faith.

Put down some roots in their company. These people believe in us, motivate us and inspire us towards a life of fruitfulness.

I learned the value of cheerleaders when I ran the London Marathon for the first time. I had been encouraged to run the race wearing a T-shirt with my name in big, bold letters across the front. I didn't fully appreciate the benefit of doing this until the end of the first mile, when a lady leaned out of the window of her apartment, high above the street, and shouted at the top of her voice, 'Go on, Duncan, you can do it!' I had never met her before and I've never seen her since, but in that moment I experienced the value of cheerleaders. In fact, for the whole of the 26.2 miles of that marathon, all I could hear was people lining the streets of London shouting my name.

We need those kinds of people in our lives. When you find one, put down some roots and stick to them like glue.

Rooted in the company of *wise counsellors*
The writer of Proverbs has plenty to say about these kinds of people.

> Walk with the wise and become wise,
> for a companion of fools suffers harm.
> (Proverbs 13:20)

The message is simple: if you want to make good decisions and live a life of wisdom, plant your life in the company of a few wise people, and uproot yourself from the company of fools. This will take intention on your part. You will need to send a message to a couple of wise people and purposefully invite them to speak into your life. I did it, and my life was better as a result.

Rooted in the company of *friends*

Many people don't need loads of close friends, but they do benefit from having a few. It's likely to be the same for you. Maybe two or three people who will walk with you on your worst days, celebrate with you on your best days, tell you the truth when you've stepped out of line and tell you if you have food stuck in your teeth. If you want to live a deep and fruitful life, it will require you to invest your life in a few friends, give them your love, and receive their love in return.

These four categories of community will require you to be intentional. So many trees thrive because they have been deliberately planted where their roots can go down deep and cause the tree to flourish.

The writer of Psalm 1 helps us visualise this principle perfectly:

> That person is like a tree planted by streams of water,
> which yields its fruit in season
> and whose left does not wither –
> whatever they do prospers.
> (Psalm 1:3)

My prayer for you, as this chapter closes, is that you will live a fruitful and abundant life (John 10:10); that the way you live, outwardly, will show that you know and love Jesus, and that you know that you are loved by Him.

And my prayer is also that you will put down deep roots that will enable that level of fruitfulness; that you will be rooted in the secret place, with the words of Jesus hidden deep in your heart, surrounded by a community of people who will play their part in seeing you thrive and grow.

> *Heavenly Father, I hide myself in You. I put my roots down in the secret place, knowing that it's there that I will feel Your heartbeat and hear Your voice. I long to be fruitful. And so I plant myself near the deep water where You are. From there I know I will thrive and grow. Amen.*

For reflection/discussion

- Take a moment to reflect on the role of unseen roots: *anchoring* and *absorbing*. What does this teach you about your life with Christ and His desire for your fruitfulness?

- Do you have a secret life with God? When is your 'best part of the day', when you can spend time in the secret place with God? How does this work with your unique schedule?

- As you reflect on being rooted in God's words, can you describe times when you have heard His voice through the things He has said and through what He is saying now?

- If your fruitfulness isn't just about who is in you, but also who is around you, list those who are your a) tribe, b) cheerleaders, c) wise counsellors and d) friends. Describe the role that each person plays. Is there one of those roles that is currently empty in your life? How could you seek out that missing person?

3

In Prayer

I entered the room, uncertain as to what would happen next. I have spent the majority of my life in churchy-type meetings and so I usually have a pretty good idea who will say and do what. I know that even non-liturgical churches actually have a liturgy. It's not written down, but there is one. I know what to expect. But this felt different.

For a few days I had joined a community that has a rhythm of prayer. Three times each day its members pause to pray. Following a set liturgy, they direct their hearts to God, and in the middle of the activities of their day they pause to remember that He's there with them.

I walked into the room, and in contrast to my own church tradition that is often noisy and energetic, this room was still. It was no less engaging; it's just that there was silence. Stillness.

And then it happened. The person leading the service welcomed everyone and invited all the people in the room to open their hands and hearts to God in prayer. Warm, heavy tears filled my eyes and uncontrollably rolled down my cheeks. No matter how hard I tried to stop them, they kept coming. I was in a room of random strangers, and I was weeping, quietly but uncontrollably.

To stop the tears, I tried to redirect my thoughts to anything else, other than what was happening in that room. Football. Food. Family. But the tears kept coming.

I tried to analyse what was occurring. I tried to make sense of it. I wasn't sure if my emotions were responding to a release of stress, as I was having a temporary break away from my leadership responsibilities, or whether my heart was responding to the presence of God in a room where, over many years, thousands of people had prayed.

One thing I know is that my tears were my prayers.

In my desire to *live deeply*, I have tried to figure out how I can emulate the lifestyle of the psalmist King David who, when encircled by ungodliness in his enemies and his own nation, declared, 'But I am in prayer' (Psalm 109:4, AMP). In that pursuit of a deeper life I have grown to understand that prayer is less about spiritual discipline and more about spiritual desire. It is birthed and it flourishes from a heart that is moved. A heart that is soft. A heart that longs. A heart that knows how to cry.

I appreciate that this kind of prayer is offensive to the strategic part of our brains because so many of us are wired for activity and productivity, and our prayers so often reflect this. We pray with a list of requests. Requests that our lives will be more efficient and less complex; that we'll have the strength to get the job done. But I've learned that the spiritual authority we need does not flow from activity but from intimacy. I've learned that before our prayers can affect the world around us, they must affect the world within us. Prayer flows from the heart. It flows from the depths. For me, when I'm most connected to the presence of God, it often starts with tears.

Praying with tears

This isn't a new concept. Many of the Bible's heroes prayed with tears. It was totally understandable that Job, after all his pain and loss, would pray with weeping. 'My eyes pour out tears to God' (Job 16:20), he said, with simple honesty.

Jeremiah's form of prayer was no different. A man who was mocked, abused and laughed at by the people he loved and served couldn't help but pray with a deep heartfelt passion for his nation.

> Oh, that my head were a spring of water
> and my eyes a fountain of tears!
> I would weep day and night
> for the slain of my people.
> (Jeremiah 9:1)

Jesus also experienced the prayer of tears. Looking over the great city of Jerusalem that He loved, 'he wept' (Luke 19:41). The tenderness of Jesus' heart meant that He would often offer up 'prayers and petitions with fervent cries and tears' (Hebrews 5:7).

The source and the purpose of our tears can be varied. Tears can flow as a response to an inward godly sorrow, as a response to a 'broken and contrite heart' (Psalm 51:17). They can flow in repentance and remorse, as an act of holy mourning. I've found that they can flow as a simple response to the tangible presence of God.

As best as I can understand it, tears are a sign that God is touching our centre. It is one way that He helps our prayers descend from our minds into our hearts. It is one way that He helps us avoid praying prayers that are theologically correct but lack feeling or emotion. While the number of literal tears we shed is not important, what is important is that we are learning to pray heartfelt prayers from deep within, from a sorrowful, repentant, thankful or joyful heart.

In my late teens, as I started to embrace a faith of my own and open my life to the presence and power of the Spirit, I found that as He did a work of grace in my heart, I just kept crying. To be honest, it was sometimes embarrassing! I would be in worship services or prayer meetings, and as hard as I tried to stop them, tears kept coming. I appreciate that people often have physical manifestations when they encounter and experience the presence of God. Some shake, some feel an inner warmth, others fall down. I experienced tears.

Since those early experiences of the Spirit, I have often found that when God comes close and He works on my heart, my emotions can be located just below the surface of my life. I've found that it doesn't take too much to trigger my tears. A song of worship. A loving family experience. A generous gift. A sermon that helps me understand God's love. An experience of the beauty of creation. These encounters with God's grace towards me result in deep, tear-filled prayers of gratitude.

You may ask, 'How do I pray with tears?' Of course, there are some forms of prayer that can be taught. I don't believe that this is one of them. I don't believe this is something you learn, but it is something you can ask for.

Ask God to break your heart so that you feel His pain for the world. Ask Him to break your heart as you fully own your sin and you offer prayers of confession and repentance. Ask God to soften your heart, to pierce your hard-heartedness with His tender-heartedness. Ask God for a sensitivity to His presence. Ask Him for tears.

I'm learning that to *live deeply* is to pray from the heart. It is to pray with desire and emotion. It is to pray with tears.

And I'm learning that to *live deeply* requires me to pray as a seeker, to pray as someone who knows that they have an inner emptiness that will only be filled when they find God.

Praying as a seeker

Early one Sunday morning, before heading towards church and preaching the sermon for that day, I went for a long run. I've often found that this routine helps clear my mind and energise my body for the responsibilities of the day ahead. In the weeks preceding, I had been praying about what I should do with the next portion of my life, and how I should lead the church I serve into a new season. I was about to take a sabbatical, and my key question entering that break was, 'God, what do You want me to do?'

Midway through my run, I paused to take a drink, and out of nowhere I sensed God speak to me. Although this wasn't an experience of the audible voice of God (something I've never heard!), His voice came as clear as it ever has done for me. I heard Him say, 'When you find

Me, you'll find out what to do.' In that moment, it felt like God was answering the prayer I had been praying repeatedly. But rather than receiving a clear answer with five steps to take into my future, I was invited into a pursuit. I was invited to seek.

The idea of *finding God* is an interesting one. It almost suggests that He is difficult to locate, as though He's hiding from us and doesn't want to be found. Nothing could be further from the truth. In fact, there are some things about God that are so easy to find that it's almost impossible for Him to hide them from us.

My wife Helen and I have four children, and because of their wide age range, I have been playing the same games with them for nearly twenty years. Many times I've played the old game of hide-and-seek around our house with one of our children, and each time I play I have the exact same problem. Where can a six-foot-one-inch man hide in an average pre-war terraced house in Coventry? If you're eight years old, you can hide in cupboards and under beds. It's not so easy when you're adult-sized! Even though my children knew that my best hiding place was to lie in the bath or hide behind the shower screen, they absolutely loved the moment that they found me. They would laugh and scream with excitement because they found someone who was kind of hidden from them.

I think there are some things about God that He almost can't hide from us. Just take a walk in the countryside and you'll soon find His beautiful creativity. Just take a look at the stars on a cloudless night and you'll soon find His majesty. Just take a look at the human body and you'll soon find His ingenious design and handiwork. We sometimes call these attributes of God a manifestation of

His omnipresence. They are difficult to hide because they are visible all around us.

But there is another aspect of God's presence that sometimes requires a little more seeking. We might call this His manifest presence. I'm talking about moments when it actually feels like He walks into the room; like He turns His face towards us; like He's standing at our side; like we're actually having a conversation with Him. It is to experience practically what we believe theologically.

Jeremiah 29 is much loved – verse 11 has been widely used on fridge magnets and screensavers:

> 'For I know the plans I have for you,' declares the LORD, 'plans to prosper you and not to harm you, plans to give you hope and a future.'

It's the kind of verse that we use to encourage other Christians that God has a plan for their life, and it's a plan to 'prosper' them, and it's a plan to give them a 'hope and a future'. These are great words.

It's worth remembering that, in context, this verse didn't promise the people immediate success. They would have to wait many decades for God to deliver them. And it places the pursuit of God and an experience of His manifest presence as something even greater than the promise of plans, purpose and prosperity. The pinnacle of this prophetic promise is that they will find God if they wholeheartedly seek Him:

> 'You will seek me and find me when you seek me with all your heart. I will be found by you,' declares the LORD.
> (Jeremiah 29:13-14)

It seems to me that those moments when we experience His manifest presence occur because two things come together at the same time: our seeking of Him and His desire to be found by us. It seems to me that if we are going to *live deeply*, we must pray as seekers, because He loves to be sought after. He waits to be wanted. There are deeper encounters with His presence that can't be experienced by a causal search. In fact, I wonder if there are aspects of His character that He hides from us, so that after the seeking we experience the delight of finding them. God points to this in Jeremiah 33:3 where He says:

> Call to me and I will answer you and tell you great
> and unsearchable things you do not know.
> (Jeremiah 33:3)

This command to seek God in prayer (and it is often a command!) is found throughout the Scriptures, most prominently in the words of King David in the Psalms. One of the things I love about the life of David is that he seemed to experience the benefits of the New Covenant in the days of the Old Covenant. He appeared to know the closeness of God's presence that was usually reserved for the high priest and wasn't made available to ordinary people until after the death and resurrection of Jesus. Yet David had a deep awareness of the Lord's manifest presence with him, and maybe that was because he knew the importance of seeking God. He would write things like:

> One thing I ask from the LORD,
> this only do I seek:

that I may dwell in the house of the LORD
all the days of my life,
to gaze on the beauty of the LORD
and to seek him in his temple.
(Psalm 27:4)

My heart says of you, 'Seek his face!'
Your face, LORD, I will seek.
(Psalm 27:8)

You, God, are my God,
earnestly I seek you;
I thirst for you,
my whole being longs for you,
in a dry and parched land
where there is no water.
(Psalm 63:1)

And it's important to note that this prayerful seeking of
God is primarily a heart matter. We find Him when we
seek Him *with all our hearts*, which is interesting because
the culture of many churches encourages people to seek
God with their minds and to study more about Him, or to
pursue Him with their works, through acts of service.
While studying and serving, thinking and doing are very
good things, the seeking of God is first a heart thing.
Something stirs in our hearts and says, 'I cannot live in
mediocrity, knowing that there's more of God to
experience and explore – and then do nothing about it!' It
starts with a longing, a passion in our hearts for
encounters with His manifest presence. Our hearts carry
the great paradox of knowing God yet knowing there's

more of Him to know. Our hearts burn to know Him more deeply.

How do we practically cultivate a heart that seeks God in prayer? My simple observation is that what we value in our hearts will be visible in our habits. There is no formation without repetition. If we have a heart to seek God, it will become evident in how we prioritise our time and in the rhythms that we adopt. Those habits will be determined by our season of life, because those with small children will have different routines from those who are retired. Those habits will be determined by our personality type, because those who are introverts will likely lean towards seeking God in solitude, while those who are extroverts will probably lean in to seeking God in community. Those habits will be determined by whether we're a lark or an owl, by whether we're wired to get up early to pray or whether we will stay up late and seek God through the night. And those habits will be determined by our church tradition, which may be contemplative or charismatic, which may mean seeking God in stillness or in the spontaneous.

I guess what I'm trying to say is this: 'Do whatever it takes! Do whatever you need to do to seek Him in prayer with all your heart!', knowing that God 'rewards those who earnestly seek him' (Hebrews 11:6).

I'm learning that if I am to *live deeply*, I must pray as a seeker. And I'm also learning that if I am to leave the shallows and enter the depths, I must pray with my eyes open.

Praying with eyes open

A little while ago I learned something new (which isn't unusual for me!). I was reading about the story of the raising of Lazarus in John 11, and the way Jesus prayed to His Father for His friend's resurrection:

> So they took away the stone. Then Jesus looked up and said, 'Father, I thank you that you have heard me. I knew that you always hear me, but I said this for the benefit of the people standing here, that they may believe that you sent me.'
> (John 11:41-42)

Rather than closing His eyes to pray (like many of us do), Jesus kept them open and prayed.

I understand that this was a common way for Jewish people to pray in those days. It reminded them that God was right there, right now, in their real world. By keeping their eyes open, it reminded them that the line between the spiritual and the physical was very thin; that the invisible God was very present with them in the physical world.

While it's important to pray with heartfelt emotion and with the all-in heart of a seeker, I've found that *living deeply* also requires a slightly less-intense form of prayer. I've started to call it 'praying with my eyes open'. It is to see God in the ordinary things of life. It is to commune with Him throughout a normal day. It is to break down the spiritual and secular divide that categorises certain aspects of my life as being of interest to the divine, whereas other parts of my life are earthly and of no concern to Him. I've been learning that my life is enriched when I live with a deeper and clearer perception of the Father's presence in the routine of my daily living.

This means that I can maintain an awareness of His presence all day long. I can be eating my muesli in the morning and be in the Father's presence. I can be on the train to work and be in the Father's presence. I can spend a day in the office and be in the Father's presence. I can be caring for elderly parents and be in the Father's presence. I can be putting my children to bed and be in the Father's presence. To *live deeply* requires me to turn my everyday, ordinary living towards God as prayer.

I can pray with my eyes open.

As I drive to work, I thank God for the provision of a car. As I plant flowers in my garden, I thank Him for the sun and the rain. As I walk through a local park, I pray a blessing over the people that I pass. As I watch the news broadcast, I pray for peace in the world. As I join the queue in my supermarket, I pray a prayer of gratitude that the shelves are stocked with food for my family to eat.

In recent months I've added an extra element to my daily routine. For fifteen minutes before going to bed, I take a brief prayer walk around my block. Sometimes I pop on some headphones and listen to a few songs of worship, but mostly I walk with and talk to the Lord. I reflect on the day and recall where I met Him and apologise for where I missed Him. I thank Him for His good gifts to me. I pray for the streets that I walk along and the homes that I pass. It's a simple way to end my day. I pray with my eyes open.

I think that we often see our ordinary, everyday lives as an obstacle to having a healthy prayer life. We think that our work life, family life and our over-committed schedule get in the way of achieving that goal. But when we pray with our eyes open, we can turn every part of our life into a prayer. Our lives become a prayer in action. The apostle Paul taught the Corinthian church:

> So whether you eat or drink or whatever you do, do
> it all for the glory of God.
> (1 Corinthians 10:31)

In effect, Paul was saying, 'Whatever you do, offer it as a prayer to God, saying, "I'm doing this for Your glory!"' This means that you can mow lawns, cut hair, teach children, repair cars, sweep streets, make coffee, input data, stock shelves, serve customers, count cash, analyse statistics, cook meals and care for patients as a prayer to God. And you can, and probably should, do all those things with your eyes open!

But I am in prayer

The world we find ourselves in can be a very dark place, with multiple distractions that lead us away from living deeply. The magnetic pull towards a lifestyle of shallowness and skimming is strong. But I want to resist that pull. I want to be like David, who found himself surrounded by ungodly distractions, even evil influences, and was able to state with boldness, 'But I am in prayer' (Psalm 109:4, AMP). I want that to be my testimony too.

> My eyes may be filled with tears, *but I am in prayer*.
> My heart may be seeking, *but I am in prayer*.
> My eyes may be open, *but I am in prayer*.

*Heavenly Father, I long for You. And this longing
is more than a mere duty; more than a discipline.
It's my deepest desire. I want to know You. I want
to see You. I want to sense You close to me. And so
I will seek after You with all my heart. Amen.*

For reflection/discussion

- Have you ever had the experience of your tears being your prayers? If so, describe what was happening in that moment.

- Reflect on your experiences of God's omnipresence and His manifest presence. How do you distinguish between the two, and what have been your encounters with each one?

- 'The seeking of God is first a heart thing.' What's the difference between seeking God with our minds and seeking Him with our hearts?

- What do you understand by the concept of 'praying with your eyes open' and how it helps you see God in the ordinary events of everyday life?

4

Mystery

Simon was just thirty-four years of age when he died. He had been one of the pastors at the church I lead, from 2009 through to 2017. For me, Simon was a bit like a spiritual son; at times it felt like we had a 'Paul with Timothy' type of relationship. When he was diagnosed with cancer, we prayed fervently that he would be healed. We trusted in God's healing power. We put our hope in Him. But Simon didn't receive his physical healing, and in November 2019 he went home to be with Jesus, leaving behind Lisa and two small children.

There's barely a day gone by that I haven't thought about him since. I run past their old family home a couple of times a week. My computer has multiple files that were Simon's files. My office and our church building contain many memories of him.

I briefly tell you that story because it raises a big question for me: 'How do you draw close to a God who doesn't do what you expect Him to do or want Him to do?' We prayed for healing, and He didn't heal; at least, not in the way we prayed for.

We all have stories like this that we could tell. It may be a story of childlessness, or bereavement, or unemployment, or bankruptcy, or long-term illness, or false accusations, or divorce. It will likely be a story of you praying and hoping and waiting. It will probably be a story of disappointment, discouragement and despair. It will be a story of broken hearts and broken lives. It will be a story of God not acting in the way you believed He would act. He was distant. Unresponsive. Unpredictable. UnGodlike (if that's a word!).

What do you do when certitude is no longer certain? How do you respond when God operates outside the box you placed Him in? What kind of faith do you have left when your faith is in a God that you cannot fully understand? Is it even possible to 'remain' with an incomprehensible God?

In my search for a deeper life and a deeper faith, I've concluded that God is not an equation to be solved. He is more like a mystery to be explored. So often our secular minds oppose the mysterious. We pursue solutions. We demand an answer to every problem. We expect every element of our life to be labelled, controlled, managed and understood, including God. But I've discovered that the solved life is a shallow life. The solved life believes that true meaning can only be found in what I fully understand. It requires that all questions must be answered. The deeper life, however, allows space for mystery. It draws us into a relationship with a Being who is eternally complex. It calls us towards a God who cannot be worked out but, mind-bogglingly, can be known.

Google has changed us. It has changed so many of our interactions. We can no longer have a casual conversation with a friend, and when we arrive at a subject where neither party agrees on the answer to a specific dilemma, or there's a debate over who is wrong or right, we can't just accept that there's no solution. Now we can Google it! It eliminates doubt and ambiguity. It gives us certitude. Within a few seconds we are provided with an answer to almost every question. The speed of light? Solved. How do I stop the hiccups? Resolved. Can I feed my pet rabbit dandelion leaves? Definitely. Will West Ham United win the Premier League title? Of course! Google provides all the answers.

Well, not all the answers.

Mysteries remain.

Oh, the depth

The apostle Paul was a great intellectual, a leading academic of his day, but he loved to speak of *mystery*. He loved to speak of the things he couldn't quite get his head around. He used that vivid word twenty-one times in his letters. Among other things, he describes the 'mystery of Christ' (Colossians 4:3), the 'mystery of the gospel' (Ephesians 6:19) and the 'mystery of God' (Colossians 2:2). Paul, with his life built on a firm foundation of theological, educational and academic pursuits, was quite content to embrace sacred mysteries. He didn't give the impression that he had to give a full explanation for every aspect of the Christian faith, turning those rich mysteries into cheap certainties. No. He was quite content to allow some things to remain mysterious. For me, Paul's embrace of mystery reaches a crescendo in his doxology of Romans 11:

Oh, the depth of the riches of the wisdom and
knowledge of God!
How unsearchable his judgments,
and his paths beyond tracing out!
(Romans 11:33)

I cast my mind back to my theological training and
preparation for pastoral, local church ministry. I recall the
thick, systematic theology books that we were instructed
to read carefully. Our studies were designed to help us to
understand God and then to pass on that knowledge, to
teach others to understand Him too. Those books told us
that God has certain attributes and perfections. That He is
A + B + C and if you pray to Him in a certain way, He'll do
D + E, and sometimes, if you have enough faith, He'll also
do F + G. My reading of this kind of book created in me a
theology where I could predict how God would act, what
He would say and do in any given situation. And then I
entered the real world.

I've begun to wonder if, at the start of any theological
training, students shouldn't first be given textbooks, but
rather they should be taken outside on a starry night and
encouraged to stare at the sky. I wonder if they should
start by considering 'your heavens ... the moon and the
stars' (Psalm 8:3). I wonder if the starting point should be
curiosity rather than *mastery*. In their pursuit of God and
the deeper life, I wonder if they should begin with holy
curiosity rather than the goal of mastering theology. I
wonder if they should start with *wonder*.

Many years ago, I attended a conference for leaders
where one of the main speakers talked about how you can
divide people into two distinct groups. He said there are

'left-brain thinkers' and 'right-brain dreamers'. He told us that the brain is made up of two halves, two distinct hemispheres. The left side is logical, analytical and practical; it sees patterns and order; it is fact- and knowledge-based. The right side is big-picture orientated; it's where you dream, imagine and see images, symbols and pictures. It's where you think of possibilities and ideas.

Apparently, in all of us, one side of the brain dominates our thinking and therefore shapes our character, personality and decision-making. It even forms our approach to faith. I checked online to see if he was telling the truth, and the internet said he was, so if the internet says it's true, it must be true!

Those dominated by the right side are dreamers; they think big, they take risks, they have great imaginations, they are creative and artistic. Those dominated by the left side are analytical, facts-based, orderly, need proof for everything; they study the details and look for patterns. In school the left-brainers lean towards maths and science, whereas the right-brainers pursue things like art, drama and music. As you read this book, if you are a left-brainer you are probably hoping that you can learn something new, but if you are a right-brainer, you are hoping that I share a load of stories that inspire you.

When Abraham was presented with the grand and impossible vision of becoming the father of a great nation, a dream that he couldn't logically understand, God didn't provide a step-by-step guide as to how He would make it happen. He invited Abraham to step out of his tent and to count the stars. In that moment, under the starry sky, Abraham was reminded of how small he was, and how big God is (Genesis 15:5). Abraham learned that God was not subject to left-brain logic.

The problem for left-brainers (of which I am one!) is that we analyse everything. We try to understand everything. We worship predictability. But what do you do when the God you worship is both dependable and unpredictable? What do you do when you spend time creating theological boxes for God, and then you discover that He is so much bigger than the boxes you created for Him? What do you do when you make 'rational argument' the entry point to a relationship with God, and then you discover that it's not possible to fully understand the God you want to believe in? What do you do when God doesn't really fit a 'fill in the blanks' sermon? What do you do when He doesn't give you the answers, He just gives you Himself? When He just says, 'remain in me' (John 15:4)?

During my recent sabbatical, I attended a number of church services and gatherings that were different from my own tradition and denomination. I attended services with a set liturgy. Along with other Christians, I read aloud prayers, statements and creeds that I hadn't read for many years. I loved this renewed experience. As I read those great ancient creeds, it struck me that I was confessing with my mouth many things that I couldn't explain with my mind. I confessed my belief in the Trinity but, in all honesty, I struggle to explain it comprehensively. I confessed my belief that Jesus, the Son of God, rose again on the third day, but I can't fully explain how that actually happened. I confessed with my mouth that one day He will come again, but despite all the charts and diagrams I've seen over the years, I don't quite know how or when that will happen. I have a theology degree. I do my best to legitimately understand and explain everything I can. But so much remains a mystery.

Being right

Assurance of faith is vital. Carrying core convictions about who Jesus is, is important. Knowing what you believe is critical. Understanding God as best you can is more than helpful. Confessing good theology is central. But there is a form of certainty that can be very cruel. There is a fundamentalist rightness that looks more like arrogance than humility. It places ego at the centre. There is a form of Christianity that appears to say to the world, 'I am right,' and allows little room for curiosity, exploration or even mystery. It doesn't allow questions. It shuts down alternative viewpoints without careful listening. It leaves us clinging to the rightness of our traditions. At its worst, it becomes dismissive, rude and inhumane; it blames a person's pain on their lack of faith rather than on the confusing and frustrating reality that bad things happen to good people; it preaches that there are certain types of people who are unable to have a loving relationship with the God who is love.

There is a certainty that is harsh and unkind. Sometimes it's downright nasty. But there is a humility that comes with embracing mystery. Mystery gives us growth language. It provides us with a way of saying, 'I know so little, and I have so much to learn.' There is a mystery that, if we choose to allow it, will lead us into childlike faith.

In the Old Testament, Job is the archetype when it comes to trusting God despite there being a thousand reasons not to do so. His life is profoundly impacted when the spiritual realm invades the physical realm. He loses everything that he loves, including members of his family that he deeply cares for. He is surrounded by friends who, in the 'rightness' of their traditions and beliefs, try to find something or someone on to which they can pin the blame for Job's tragedy. They look for an answer that they can hold on to because it's impossible for them to have a faith without an answer. No answers – no faith.

Job is different. He eventually sits quietly in the presence of mystery and says, 'Though He slay me, yet will I trust Him' (Job 13:15, NKJV). Anyone can trust God when there are adequate answers. The person who lives deeply and knows God intimately has found a way to be close to God even when there are multiple reasons for walking away.

This I know

Why did Simon die? I don't know. It remains a mystery to me. Why do hardworking people lose their jobs? I don't know. Why do good people get sick? I don't know. Why do people who pray for a family never conceive? I don't know. Why do some evil people never have to pay for their crimes? I don't know. Why doesn't God step in and remove all injustice, poverty, hunger and abuse? I don't know.

So much remains a mystery to me.

But there are some things I do know.

I know that I should be slow to give quick and clever answers.

I know that God is not troubled by my honest doubts.

I know that it's unhealthy to spend my life critiquing God.

I know that there is a love that is so great that it is incomprehensible to the human mind.

I know that the Spirit blows wherever He wants (John 3:8), and He cannot be contained by my systematic theology.

I know that the process of knowing God deeply begins when I realise how little I really know Him.

I know that know-it-all fundamentalism never satisfies the longings of the human soul.

I know that I am formed by my holy curiosity.

I know that I can allow my 'Why?' to take me deeper into God, rather than take me away from Him.

I know that there is a peace available to me that transcends my understanding (Philippians 4:7).

I know that Jesus Christ dwells in my heart. I remain in Him. He remains in me. And I know that *living deeply* requires me to lean into and embrace the sacredness of this profound mystery.

> *Heavenly Father, there are so many things in my life that I struggle to understand. Some of those things frustrate me, some have made me angry, others have caused me to be very sad. But I'm learning to trust You in the mystery. I'm learning to embrace the greatest mystery of all – that You live in my heart and that You love me from there. Amen.*

For reflection/discussion

- Reflect on the statement, 'God is not an equation to be solved. He is more like a mystery to be explored.' What does this mean to you?

- How do you understand the difference between 'curiosity' and 'mastery' when it comes to our relationship with God?

- What are your experiences of God being both dependable and unpredictable?

- What are the positives and negatives of being certain? Are there specific dangers in our desire to be 'right'?

SECTION TWO

CONTINUING

Living like Jesus

5

Go Low

The email arrived on Monday morning. It was the day after we had hosted a well-known and well-respected guest preacher. Like many visiting ministers do, he was writing to express his gratitude for the opportunity to speak at our church. As he concluded his delightfully worded email, he signed off with a final sentence that went something like this: 'Duncan, I've noticed something about your leadership that I think needs some work, and if you give me a call, I'll talk to you about it and I'll help you improve.'

Now, you might like to think that the first thought that came into my mind was, 'Tell me more. I love people showing me how I can get better at my job!' But that's not how it went. My first thought went something like this: 'How dare he! Who does he think he is?'

The ego and the pride that resided deep in my heart quickly found their way to the surface, and feelings, thoughts and words of self-defence overflowed.

Thankfully, I have learned not to respond to those kinds of emails too quickly, and during the next forty-eight hours, as the email sat in my inbox, the Holy Spirit began to work on my interior world. My response slowly changed to, 'How dare I! Who do I think I am?' My heart began to soften, my arrogance gradually melted and I called the esteemed guest preacher, withheld from him my initial reaction and told him I was keen to learn. His advice, given more than fifteen years ago, still helps me to be a better leader and communicator today. In reality, my pride could have easily got in the way of my growth.

The pathway to the deeper life is a downward one. In a selfie-centred world, it requires us to aggressively confront our ego and choose a life of humility. In a culture of narcissism and self-absorption that has infected almost every stratum of society, from world leaders in the corridors of power to everyday people posting everyday social media posts, we follow a Man on a cross.

Jesus' rule change

Jesus changed the scorecard. He moved the goalposts. It's not that He was anti-ambition. He actually called His followers to actively pursue greatness. Not the kind of greatness that jostles for position and stands on others in order to climb to the top of the tree; His was a form of greatness that would take one downward step after another. The hero in Jesus' kingdom was not the person at the summit, but the person at base camp helping others climb ahead of them.

Sports Day was always a highlight during my primary school education. Once a year, squeezed between the boredom of maths, English and science lessons, the whole school gathered on the grass playing fields to compete for the eternal glory that was given to those who were strong enough and fast enough to win a race. Of course, there were the usual running races and then the slightly less-than-Olympic-standard races that required participants to carry an egg on a spoon, or run with a leg attached to a classmate, or move as fast as they could with both legs restricted by a sack that had previously housed potatoes.

Our school added a slightly unique event. The slow bike race. Contestants were asked to bring their bicycles from home; they rode them to the starting line and when they were told to 'go', they did their best to stand still. Racers were disqualified if they put a foot down, so they would inch forward just enough to keep their bikes balanced. The winner's prize was awarded to the last person to cross the finishing line. The loser? The first person to cross that same line.

Imagine participating in that race but no one has told you the rules. When the race starts, you naturally pedal as fast as you can, you get out of breath, you break into a sweat, you are first over the line, you are the winner! At least, that's what you think, until someone explains the rules to you.

Jesus switched the rules. For almost all of us they will initially feel counterintuitive. In an ego-dominated world where arrogance and boasting are normalised, we run as servants. In a culture of self-promotion and self-congratulation, Jesus' playbook tells us to lower ourselves and 'walk humbly with [our] God' (Micah 6:8). Radical new rules.

Into an honour–shame culture, where much of life was focused on the receiving of public praise and the avoidance of public shame, Jesus was born in a manger.

The King of the Jews entered the world as a weak and powerless infant at the exact same time that another self-proclaimed king of the Jews was violently clinging to power. The first King would lay down His life in an act of self-sacrifice; the second, Herod, would oppress the weak, abuse his power and use aggression to achieve his goals.

Jesus enters the world wrapped in swaddling bands and leaves the world wrapped in a servant's towel. He changes the scorecard, switches the rules and establishes a new pattern for living.

Jesus is not just perfect in His power and His love. He is perfect in His humility. We rightly celebrate that God is omnipotent, omniscient and omnipresent. We marvel at His holiness, but we must not ignore His humility. The way we sometimes talk about God makes Him sound like a divine narcissist, driven by a desire for our undivided attention. He is nothing like that. He is driven by love, and that love is expressed through His humility. While it may be an abhorrent concept to adherents of other religions, the God of Christianity is humble. It almost sounds like blasphemy, until we join in with the apostle Paul's ancient hymn, written clearly on the pages of our Bible, that Jesus:

> … being in very nature God,
> did not consider equality with God something to be
> used to his own advantage;
> rather, he made himself nothing
> by taking the very nature of a servant,
> being made in human likeness.
> And being found in appearance as a man,
> he humbled himself
> by becoming obedient to death –

even death on a cross!
(Philippians 2:6-8)

These beautiful Pauline words are preceded by a statement that should cause us all to sit up and take note: 'have the same mindset as Christ Jesus' (Philippians 2:5). Paul's words were not just written so that we would be inspired to admire and worship Jesus, although that's obviously a very good thing to do. They were written to change the way we live. They were written to call us deeper. They were written to teach us that it's impossible to live deeply without first living humbly.

Defining humility

Forming a definition of humility is a bit like trying to hold a piece of wet soap in your hands. As soon as you think you've got hold of it, it slips out of your grip. It can be found somewhere in that awkward tension of being 'fearfully and wonderfully made' (Psalm 139:14), while also being created 'from the dust of the ground' (Genesis 2:7). It's the same with living a humble life. As soon as you think you're making progress, you realise that there are previously unexplored compartments of your character that are difficult to get under control.

It is worth, however, offering four characteristics of humility that will help us identify it when we see it:

Valuable
While the original languages of the Bible would remind us that the meaning of humility is found in our origins in the dust and dirt of the earth, it would be wrong to interpret

this as a lack of worth or dignity. Since humility requires a person to lower themselves, it presupposes that they are acting from 'height' and that they have a healthy sense of their own value. They know that they have been made 'in the image of God' (Genesis 1:27) and they can celebrate the gifts, talents and strengths that they have been given.

Intentional
Humility is not a spiritual gift given by God. It is a choice. In the same way Jesus 'humbled himself', the deeper life is reserved for those who will resist the magnetic pull of our egocentric culture and through personal choice will humble themselves. Thus, the person who is humble cannot be humiliated because they have already decided to forgo their status and, in an act of subversive rebellion towards the prevailing culture, they have intentionally demoted themselves.

Relational
Humility is not a private act of self-deprecation performed by a hermit living apart from a community. Humility is the redirecting of a person's strengths for the good of others. The humble person resists the temptations of competition and comparison, and they actively promote others in their stead, rejoicing in others' successes ahead of their own.

Liberating
Humility is freedom. It releases us from the burden of standing on centre stage. We are freed from always needing to be right, always having to be perfect and always needing to perform. It frees us from the need to be

known, to be appreciated, recognised and thanked. For the humble person, the pressure's off!

Jesus at the centre (not me!)

In essence, the heart of humility is found in the statement that almost every parent has made to their tantrum-throwing child when they don't get what they want: 'The whole world does not revolve around you!'

It's the similar discovery that the sixteenth-century Polish astronomer Nicolaus Copernicus made that rocked the then known world. Until that point in time, many of the inhabitants of the earth believed that all the planets, including the sun, were in orbit around the earth. They believed that we were smack bang at the centre of the universe. To the horror of many, he discovered that the earth was not at the centre at all, and that we were in fact orbiting the sun. He had to controversially declare that the whole universe did not revolve around us!

Just before I celebrated twenty-five years of pastoral ministry, the majority of that time spent as the senior pastor of one church, I was generously provided with a three-month sabbatical. Up until that point I hadn't always been very good at switching off from my work, and even when on holiday I would be regularly checking my emails and messages. It was a bad and unhealthy habit. Somewhere in my heart I had believed the lie that in my absence the church wouldn't function properly, people would stop attending, offerings would go down and everything would fall apart if I wasn't in control. How arrogant!

On sabbatical I switched off everything for three months. No emails. No WhatsApp groups. No messages. Guess what happened? Nothing! The church functioned perfectly in my absence. People continued attending. People kept on giving. The church thrived as well in my absence as it did in my presence. It was a lesson in humility. I quickly learned that the church does not revolve around me. In fact, I had to face the reality that Jesus is the Head of the Church, that He will build His Church, and whether I'm involved or not is in a sense irrelevant, because He is at the centre, not me.

Humility requires you to make this painful discovery too: the world does not revolve around you. You were made from the dust. To the dust you will return. And in your absence, God will get on just fine looking after the world without your help!

I am not the Messiah

The temptation to promote ourselves is as old as the Garden. The whisper of the snake still makes its way through our ear gate and into our hearts: 'You will be like God' (Genesis 3:5). We subconsciously usurp God's unique claim to omnipotence, omniscience and omnipresence. To anyone who will listen, we foolishly give the impression that we have unlimited energy, that we have the answer to every question and that we can be in more than one place at a time. We can easily adopt a messiah complex, supposing that we can fix people and fix situations. We can fall into the trap of believing that we are solely responsible for rescuing, saving or healing those who are lost or broken. Such thinking is pure ego.

We embrace the deeper life when we humbly admit that just because we are in Christ, we are not invincible. That we have substantial limitations. That we are not the Messiah!

John the Baptist got this one right. He knew who he was, and he knew who he wasn't. When large crowds started to flock to listen to him, he could have easily exaggerated his achievements and overstated his identity. He could have engaged his ego, but instead he chose the downward path of humility.

> He did not fail to confess, but confessed freely, 'I am not the Messiah.'
>
> They asked him, 'Then who are you? Are you Elijah?'
>
> He said, 'I am not.'
>
> 'Are you the Prophet?'
>
> He answered, 'No.'
>
> Finally they said, 'Who are you? Give us an answer to take back to those who sent us. What do you say about yourself?'
>
> John replied in the words of Isaiah the prophet, 'I am the voice of one calling in the wilderness, "Make straight the way for the Lord."'
> (John 1:20-23)

That's humility right there. It's not minimising your calling and your gifts. In fact, knowing your purpose and identifying your God-given talents can help bring clarity and confidence to your life. John was clear: 'I'm here to create a path for the Messiah to come. But I'm not Him.

I'm not the Messiah!' In fact, 'He must become greater; I must become less' (John 3:30).

In case you didn't know, you are not God. You are not the Messiah. You are just soil with a soul. Humility starts there.

'Raise your profile'

As I look back to my first employed position, even though I was accepted on to a management training programme, in reality I was the bank's office junior, as I mentioned previously. Every day was packed full of photocopying, filing and making hot drinks for the senior management team. Not the most exciting role I've ever played! One day my manager called me into his office to let me know that he had noticed my hard work and that I was being offered a promotion, with one caveat: I needed to 'raise my profile'. I was nineteen years old at the time and I had no idea what he meant. I didn't even know that I had a profile to raise.

Many years on from that experience, I now understand what he was communicating. 'Duncan, you need to let everyone see how good you are at your job. You need to push yourself forward more often. You need to stop hiding in the stationery cupboard, and you need to be seen!'

How different is the pattern of living that Jesus lays out for us. In a world of self-promotion, He calls us to be comfortable with anonymity. When we compete for platforms and spotlights, He tells us to be unfazed by seasons of obscurity. When our obsession with success and our drive to impress overflows into a narcissistic massaging of statistics and self-absorbed social media posts, Jesus tells us that being loved is enough.

In fact, the only time that God will rise to oppose you is when you choose the path of arrogance, because He always 'opposes the proud' (James 4:6). He will not oppose you because you have failed Him. He will not oppose you in your repentance. But He will take a stand against you in your pride.

As I've wrestled with the many ego-centred temptations of self-promotion that leaders face, I've adopted a mantra that I've returned to time and time again: *I will take care of my depth, and trust God to take care of my breadth.*

Rather than vying for opportunities to speak, preach or lead, I will leave that to God. Instead of exalting myself, I will wait for God to promote me as and when He sees fit. My job is to humble myself. His job, should He so choose, is to 'lift [me] up in due time' (1 Peter 5:6; see also James 4:10). My job is to remain teachable. To be open to correction. To laugh at myself. To stop taking myself too seriously. To reject entitlement and to see everything I have as a gift. To move in the opposite spirit to the world, and allow Him to determine how much, or how little, influence I will have.

I will just take care of my depth.

Loves to be first

There are many Bible characters who only get one mention in Scripture. In contrast to the great heroes of our faith who receive multiple references, like Moses, Joshua, Mary and Paul, these individuals get one shot at entering the biblical record. Their names are logged in history, but for some, it's not necessarily for a good reason.

Demas is simply remembered as a man who 'loved this world' (2 Timothy 4:10).

Alexander the metal worker did Paul a 'great deal of harm' (2 Timothy 4:14).

Diotrephes? Well, he 'loves to be first' (3 John 9).

Imagine being a first-century follower of a humble Messiah and then being known as the person who wants to be front and centre. Imagine seeing Jesus lay down His life as a sacrifice and then being known as someone who lives for the applause of people.

Imagine being a twenty-first-century follower of Jesus and choosing self-promotion over humble submission. Imagine making Jesus your Lord and your Leader but wanting to be first.

To live deeply is to live humbly. It is to find joy in last place; to discover the freedom of self-forgetfulness; to rejoice in new rules. It is to 'go low' because that's the path that Jesus chose.

> *Heavenly Father, I hear Your call to follow Jesus down the path of humility. I release to You any desire in me to be the centre of attention; my desire to be noticed and known. Forgive my pride. From this point on, I will pursue a different form of greatness. I will choose to go low. Amen.*

For reflection/discussion

- Since Jesus encourages us to pursue greatness, how do we balance healthy ambition with His definition of true greatness?

- What are your initial thoughts when you read that God is humble? How do you balance your understanding of His humility with His desire for His people to worship Him?

- Create your own definition of humility. How does that definition reflect the reality that we are dust that has been made in the image of God?

- How do you know that you're growing in humility? What are the markers of your progress?

6

Feel the Feelings

We left the cinema without talking. The movie had stirred something in our hearts that we were finding difficult to express. We sat in the car and I started to cry. Uncontrollably. It was 2016. The film was *Lion*,[5] an uplifting biopic about a little boy who grew up in extreme poverty in India, was tragically separated from his parents, was adopted by a family from Australia and, twenty-five years later, miraculously located his village and was reunited with his family. As I reflected on this beautiful story of redemption and restoration, something happened in my heart. The tears kept flowing. It started to get a bit embarrassing. I'm a middle-aged man, and I was worried that Helen might have thought I was having a midlife meltdown! But it wasn't anything remotely like that.

In the years preceding, Helen and I had felt God's invitation to care for some children in our city who were disadvantaged, vulnerable and sometimes unloved. This prompting led us to become foster carers and then

---

[5] *Lion*, 2016. Directed by Garth Davis.

adoptive parents, making a lifelong commitment to one child whom we love deeply.

Around the same time, our church had been building strong links with an international Christian charity that works hard to release children from poverty. We had begun to sponsor children in Ethiopia, and I had recently had the privilege of visiting our sponsored child in her home just outside Addis Ababa. These sponsored children represented more than a financial transaction; our church started to see them as part of our church family. Our sponsorship became an expression of our love.

As I remained seated in that car in 2016, I realised that my tears were more than a response to a heart-warming film. They connected to a passion in my heart. A passion for children who needed a father's love.

Those tears came from somewhere deep.

Redeeming emotions

Emotions have a bad reputation in the Christian Church. For those of us who belong to local churches that might be classified as being 'happy clappy', we tend to be criticised for being overemotional. People who raise their hands, dance expressively, sing loudly and pray with tears in their eyes can't be trusted. They are getting carried away. Too much emotion.

And then the kind of love that we preach is a 'decision love'. It's a non-emotional, reliable love. It doesn't change with our changing moods. It's a sacrificial love that isn't based on feelings. We talk about this as the highest form of love, as though adding emotion will only devalue it.

And when it comes to decision-making, we counsel people not to trust their emotions. They will confuse us or mislead us. We need to process our thinking through a logical framework. Our hearts will only deceive, not inform us.

And then we talk to people about their identity. We encourage people to know who they are, but not to base this assessment on their feelings. If they fall for that trap, one day they might feel that they are loved. The next day, not loved.

I appreciate the danger of overemotionalism. I appreciate the weakness of a form of love that shifts like the weather patterns. I appreciate the danger of, 'If it feels good, do it!' But there has to be a way to redeem our emotions and not be afraid of where they might lead us. We have to recognise the difference between embracing, even celebrating, our emotions and being controlled by them. In fact, what if the call to live deeply requires us to search below the surface and feel the feelings that God has purposefully planted in our hearts?

Jesus wept

In my early thirties, after a few years of little physical exercise, I was starting to feel quite sluggish. I'd heard people say that in order to get energy you needed to expend energy, so I started to run. My first attempt to complete a small circuit of the streets where I lived ended with heavy breathing and a puddle of sweat. But over time, my fitness increased, and eventually I started to take on the challenge of running marathons, which I began to enjoy. Strange way to find pleasure, I know.

Running a marathon requires you to cope with waves of pain. Once you reach mile twenty and you have 6.2 miles to run, your body repeatedly tells you to quit. In order to deal with those moments, and to keep moving forward, you learn to disassociate. You disconnect from the pain by focusing your mind on anything but the pain you're feeling. You think about the weather. You count to a hundred. You think about the plot of your favourite film. For me, I tend to write sermons in my head. You do whatever it takes to disassociate from the discomfort.

So many of us have learned to do the same. Not when we run, but when we live. There are pressures placed on us all to suppress certain feelings. Our family of origin, our gender, our environment and our culture create expectations as to which emotions are appropriate to express. It's acceptable for women to express sadness but not anger. It's appropriate for men to express anger but not sadness. Some societies disassociate from their grief and maintain a 'stiff upper lip'. Other cultures suppress joy because if they are caught laughing it may appear that they aren't taking their lives seriously enough. Many of us are taught to place a lid on how we feel, and not let those feelings spill out.

But Jesus was emotional.

It's wrong to see Him as a Stoic.

He was a 'man of sorrows' (Isaiah 53:3, NLT; see also Matthew 26:38).

Jesus' friend has died. Surely Lazarus was too young to have been placed in a tomb. He had so many years of life ahead of him. Years of adventure. Years with his family.

But his life has been cut short through serious illness, and so Jesus stands at the entrance of His friend's tomb, tears rolling down His face. His heart deeply moved. The emotion of the moment overtakes Him. We don't fully know why. Maybe He's feeling the pain of those who are mourning. Maybe He's experiencing the pain of personal grief. Maybe He's sad because He knows that He's just about to call His friend back from the perfection of Paradise! All we know is that Jesus feels the grief in His gut. He doesn't quash it. He doesn't disconnect from it.

'Jesus wept' (John 11:35).

But He doesn't limit His emotional repertoire to the melancholic. Jesus feels joy. He sends out seventy-two trained disciples to continue His mission and ministry in surrounding towns and villages. On their return they overflow with joy as they describe their miraculous and supernatural experiences. Jesus joins in with their celebration, 'full of joy through the Holy Spirit' (Luke 10:21). There's no suggestion that He quashes their happiness because it's irreverent or too causal. He encourages and embraces the feelings of delight. Jesus is joyful.

I wonder if Jesus had learned to express His feelings through the songs that He sang. His songbook, the Old Testament book we call Psalms, is full of emotion. In Psalm 13:2 David sings, 'day after day [I] have sorrow in my heart,' while adding a few lines later that 'my heart rejoices in your salvation' (Psalm 13:5). Just like Jesus, sorrow and joy coexist in David's heart.

Sorrow and joy

In the UK there are many things that divide us, but for decades one of our greatest divisions has centred on one controversial product. It's a sticky, salty, dark-brown paste that's packed full of B vitamins. Some will religiously smear it on every piece of toast they consume, while others won't even let it touch their lips. Marmite. Some love it. Others hate it. It divides the nation!

In fact, Marmite is so divisive that we even use the name of the product as an adjective to describe a person or an issue that divides opinion. Something or someone that some love and others hate. We say that they are 'Marmite'.

The Old Testament contains a fascinating Marmite moment. The book of Ezra describes how a group of exiles returned from captivity to Jerusalem. They were led by Zerubbabel who had it in his heart to rebuild Solomon's glorious temple that had been destroyed by the Babylonians. After a stuttering start, the foundation was laid, but rather than it soliciting an all-out celebration, there was a mixed response.

Some people brought out their trumpets and cymbals and they sang their favourite song, 'He is good; his love towards Israel endures for ever' (Ezra 3:11). They looked forward with great optimism, believing that their future would be greater than their past. They threw a party.

Other people had a more muted response. They grieved. They mourned. They were heartbroken because they could see that the new temple wouldn't be as big and grand as the first one. They saw that the temple was being downsized. They wept for what they had lost.

Ezra tells us that the cry that emerged from the community was difficult to define. It was a sound of joy and a sound of sorrow. Those who cheered, cheered at the top of their voices. Those who wept, wept with great distress (Ezra 3:13). Some celebrated their new opportunities. Others mourned their losses. There's no suggestion from the text that one group got it right and the other group got it wrong. It just tells us that there was a mixture of joy and sorrow in one place.

Do you ever feel like that? Like you have joy and sorrow in your heart at the same time? I've often found that those two opposing emotions coexist in my heart. Sometimes I feel them in my heart on the same day. Sometimes in the same hour. Sometimes in the exact same moment. It's like I experience Ezra 3 in me!

But rather than suppressing my emotional contradictions, I have learned to embrace them. I've learned that living deeply will require me to be 'sorrowful, yet always rejoicing' (2 Corinthians 6:10). I've learned that to follow Jesus means that I will share in His suffering, while also sharing in His joy (Romans 8:17; 1 Peter 4:13).

And I've learned to ask questions of those opposing feelings. Why am I feeling joyful? *What desire in me is being fulfilled?* Why am I feeling sorrowful? *What desire in me is being blocked?* I've learned that our emotions are a little like the visible part of an iceberg, and if we dive below the surface, we discover our deeper desires. Our emotion might be anger, but our desire is for justice. Our feeling might be lust, but our desire is to be loved. Our emotion might be jealousy, but our desire is to feel secure. In

Gethsemane, Jesus' emotion was sorrow, but His desire was to do His Father's will (Matthew 26:36-46). If we suppress our emotions and bury our feelings, we may never uncover the deep work God is doing and the desires He's placed into our interior world.

Everyone has a story

(and it's not the same as yours!)

It's important to add that the embracing of our feelings is not only good for our own emotional and spiritual health. It is much more than naval-gazing and a process of interior examination. We feel our feelings in order to feel the feelings that others feel; to grow in our capacity to be present to others and their emotions.

In recent years I've had to grow in this area. As a tall, white, male leader I've come to terms with the reality that there have been privileges that have been afforded to me that aren't given to others. My height, my ethnicity, my gender and my position have provided me with an inequitable advantage. My story is not the story of others. Others have stories of prejudice, injustice, bigotry and bias. They have walked into rooms and not felt welcome.

In the context of our church community, I had to face the hard truth that we had celebrated our diversity while ignoring the disparity of our lived experiences. I hadn't stopped long enough to listen; to ask questions, not for information but as an attempt to appreciate what the other person had been through; to hear someone's pain, and not make an assumption that I understood; to follow Jesus, who asked so many more questions than He gave answers, first because He wanted people to think, and second because He wanted to understand people's experiences, not just fix their pain.

When speaking to those who have been through such mistreatment, I've learned not to say, 'I know what you're going through,' because I don't. I now understand how foolish it is to place the template of my experience onto their lives. They have a story, and it's not mine. And I've learned not to offer a competing story. Previously, when someone shared with me their parenting struggles, I would listen and then talk about the time we had three children under the age of five, almost adding, 'Beat that!'

An awareness of our own emotions creates a starting point for loving others well. It acknowledges that we all have pain, it's just that we don't express it or experience it in the same way. A mature person who is aware of their own feelings can create a safe place where others can be vulnerable and honest. They are able to acknowledge that we are all beautifully made in the image of God, while also incredibly broken. If we can name our own complex feelings and fractured emotions, we create space for others to name theirs too.

So often we place an expiry date on people's grief. After a couple of months of sadness, we unkindly suggest that they begin to 'move on'. But when we've embraced our own sorrow and processed our own losses, we're not in such a rush to move others forward.

Of course, in the same way that there's a danger with disassociation, where we disconnect from our feelings and shut down, so there's an equal danger which we call enmeshment – when we dispense with healthy boundaries and we carry other people's emotions like they are our own; when our own mood becomes closely linked to another person's emotional state. People who are enmeshed call it empathy, but really it becomes co-dependency.

We see this all the time.

When parents transfer their fears on to their child before sending them on a school trip, and then the child carries those fears with them for the whole trip. When a friend shares their anxieties and the other person carries those anxieties like they belong to them too; the two friends become emotionally fused. When team members don't feel at liberty to express their own thoughts or emotions, but instead one person speaks for everyone. That's enmeshment.

There is a third way. It's known as 'differentiation', which I've heard defined as 'knowing where I end and you begin'. It is to be fully yourself, while remaining fully connected to people. A differentiated person will be deeply concerned for their anxious friend but will remain a non-anxious presence in the relationship because they realise that taking on their friend's anxiety isn't going to help them.

Consider Jesus walking the road to Emmaus with the two grieving disciples whose hearts have been broken and hopes lost. Jesus is aware of His own emotions, but as He walks with them, He isn't infected by their anxieties. He does, though, remain connected to them in their grief. He could immediately fix them. He could reveal Himself to them and heal their grief in an instant. Instead, He waits until 'their eyes [are] opened' (Luke 24:31). That's differentiation. Emotionally aware. Emotionally connected. Emotionally separate.

Feel the feelings

Just to reassure you, I don't make it a habit to sit in my car crying, but there was one more time.

At the start of the COVID-19 pandemic, a lady from our church community sadly passed away. Doris had been the cleaner at the church when I first started working there back in 1997. Even though she was thirty-five years my senior, we became friends. Like many of those who died in the early days of the pandemic, the events surrounding her death were heart-breaking because her family were unable to be at her bedside in her final moments. And then, at her funeral service, only six members of her family were permitted to attend. It was painfully sad.

Over the past few decades I've conducted many funerals. I've learned to be professional and control my emotions. This service felt different. After leaving the chapel, I found myself in my car doing something I hadn't done after a funeral for many years.

I wept.

My heart was full of sadness.

I couldn't keep the sorrow locked inside.

But that's OK because I'm learning to live deeply.

I've learned to feel the feelings.

Heavenly Father, I want to feel what You feel for our world; to allow sorrow and joy to have a place in my heart. Where I have shut down and disconnected, I reconnect and allow my redeemed emotions to draw me closer to You and the people that You love. Where I have disposed of appropriate boundaries, allowing my emotions to become enmeshed with the emotions of another, I repent. Father, I want my heart to be made healthy and whole. Amen.

For reflection/discussion

- How has your family of origin, gender, ethnicity, culture or church background influenced your expressions of emotion?

- Reflect on Jesus' expressions of emotion. What do they teach us about the appropriate place that emotion can have in our lives?

- In what ways is it helpful for you to accept that opposing emotions can coexist in the human heart?

- What do you understand to be the difference between disassociation, enmeshment and differentiation? Which of these three do you tend to drift towards when you find yourself in emotionally charged situations?

7

Loosen Your Grip

The young instructor told me to lean back, walk slowly down the side of the cliff face and trust the rope. It was my first experience of abseiling. My only experience of abseiling. Once was enough. I was a youth leader, trying my best to demonstrate an adventurous spirit to a group of young people I was leading. Unfortunately, my courage was in short supply. I had listened to the safety briefing. I had carefully watched the instructor model how we should descend the precipice. I had bought into the idea that this was going to be an exhilarating experience I would never forget. And then I had to let go. Instead, I froze. My feet refused to move. My sweaty hands gripped tighter. I was going nowhere. No amount of coaxing or cajoling was going to make a difference. There was no way I was going to entrust my life to a flimsy piece of rope. So I quit.

While this event actually happened to me, the images that this story conjure up are more important because they provide us with a metaphor for living deeply. There is a central dynamic to the deeper life that demands a willingness to surrender; to loosen our grip; to relinquish our attempts to control everything and everyone; to let go and 'lean back', abandoning ourselves to the will of God and entrusting our lives into His hands, believing that He is orchestrating everything for our good, His glory and the good of the world.

Easier said than done.

He was led

Back in 2004 I was invited to watch an advance screening of Mel Gibson's *The Passion of the Christ*. A brutal depiction of the physical suffering of Jesus as He sacrificially offers His life on the cross for the salvation of the world. The word 'passion' confused me, though. I had heard some churches refer to 'Holy Week' as 'Passion Week', but because of the types of churches I grew up in, this terminology was new to me.

I understood 'passion' to mean enthusiastic, energetic or even emotional. And while those words may have described Jesus' ministry well, they didn't seem to be a perfect fit when it came to labelling His final week and His journey to the cross.

I dug a bit deeper.

I discovered that the word 'passion' has a link to our word 'passive'. I uncovered the reality that en route to Calvary, Jesus passively absorbed something rather than actively did something. We usually think of Jesus as a 'doer'. We think about His activity. He preaches. He heals. He travels. He leads. For three years Jesus has a very active public life. But from the moment that He falls to His knees in the Garden of Gethsemane and prays with a sorrow-filled heart, Jesus stops doing things and things start to be done to Him.

It may be the only time Jesus receives a 'no' to one of His prayers. As blood-infused sweat falls from His brow, He asks, 'My Father, if it is possible, may this cup be taken from me. Yet not as I will, but as you will' (Matthew 26:39). The Father rejects the Son's request. The Son, in turn, surrenders to the will of His Father.

From that point on, Jesus is arrested, beaten, humiliated, whipped, stripped of His clothes, taken to the high priest, taken to Pilate and nailed to a cross. Jesus absorbs what is done to Him. He submits to the will of others. He submits to the will of His Father.

'He was led like a lamb to the slaughter' (Isaiah 53:7).

'Then they led him out to crucify him' (Mark 15:20).

The greatest leader to ever walk this planet was led by someone else. The One who led crowds of people who followed Him wherever He went was led away to His death. Rather than fighting back, He submitted to their leading.

How could Jesus have done that? How could He resist the temptation to regain control? Let me propose an answer: Jesus had already died before He died.

Jesus had crucified His will before He arrived at the cross. He had loosened His grip on His life. The Son had already surrendered His life in the Garden when He willingly prayed to His Father, 'Yet not as I will, but as you will.'

Jesus shows us how the surrendered life creates a route out of the shallows and into the depths.

The prayer of relinquishment

There are forms of prayer that take us deeper.

Often our prayers start with requests. These are the 'my will be done on earth' kinds of prayer. Jesus encouraged this. Our prayers for 'daily bread' (Matthew 6:11) are legitimate. Our Father loves to give us good gifts and so He welcomes our requests. But there are other prayers that plunge us into the depths. We call them 'prayers of relinquishment', and these prayers don't come easily. We wrestle with our heart's desire for power and control. We fight with our innate longing to be seen and heard, to be front and centre, to have our will be done. But the wrestle is worth it, because when we relinquish control and pray 'your will be done' (Matthew 6:10), it changes us deeply. In fact, it's probably one of the most dangerous and freeing prayers we can pray.

Have you noticed that there are some people who make terrible passengers on car journeys? Maybe you're one of them! They sit there without a steering wheel, but they wriggle around in that seat unable to camouflage their discomfort with their lack of control! Their right foot presses the imaginary brake pedal. Their inability to control their own destiny creates an uneasiness that seeps into the atmosphere of the whole car. Sound familiar?

What happens in the car happens in the heart. We want to control outcomes. We want to control the future of our families, our finances, our friendships. We have hopes, dreams and ambitions that we cling to, not wanting to risk letting go of those things that mean so much to us. And yet, maintaining control only creates more pressure: the pressure to get everything right, the burdens of performance and perfection, the anxiety of carrying responsibility. These weigh heavily on the human heart. But a freedom is found when we offer up prayers of relinquishment.

Every few months I meet with a spiritual director. He's an older gentleman who helps me notice God's activity in my life as I share with him details of my life and spiritual journey. His role is not to give advice, just to ask some probing questions that provoke me to see what God might be saying to me or doing in me, especially when I've been too distracted to listen or notice. Sometimes we talk for an hour. Other times we sit in silence together and wait to see what God might reveal.

Recently I was sharing with him about some of my leadership responsibilities. I was telling him that I don't always enjoy the demands of being a leader, and that the weight of responsibility often feels too heavy for me to carry. After a long pause, he looked at me with caring eyes and said, 'Duncan, I've noticed that you keep talking about "my responsibilities" and I'm wondering if you should start to see them as "God's responsibilities"?' It was like he had fired an arrow directly into the bullseye of my heart. My eyes were opened to a new way of seeing my life.

Straight after that meeting, I sat in the stillness of my car and I prayed a prayer of relinquishment that went something like this: 'Father, I release into Your hands all my responsibilities. Do with them what You will, when You will, as You will. I give over to You my need to be in control, my desire to impress and my self-imposed pressure to perform. My responsibilities are no longer mine. I give them to You because You'll do a better job than me anyway! Amen.'

The cruciform life

The deeper life is the cruciform life. It is a life formed in the shadow of the cross. It forgoes the things we crave: prominence, attention, comfort and control. It entrusts outcomes to the Father. Not my will but His will be done.

Back in 2015 a story hit the news that twenty-one Egyptian Christian labourers had been captured by Islamic State (IS) in Libya. They were beheaded on a beach, with the film of this terrible event being circulated around the world.[6] As I heard that tragic story, a question came into my mind: 'How did they know they were Christians?' As I read more widely, I discovered that many Egyptian Christians are part of the Coptic Church, one of the world's oldest denominations, and early on in childhood they are given a tattoo on their wrist – the tattoo of a cross. It was quite possible that this tattoo marked out those twenty-one martyrs as Christians. It is woven into Coptic Christianity that to follow Jesus is to be shaped by the cross and to live in its shadow.

I'm reminded of the apostle Paul's words to the Colossian church: 'For you died, and your life is now hidden with Christ in God' (Colossians 3:3). A strange thing to write to a group of people whose hearts are still beating and their lungs are still full of air! The stark reality is that, when you read through much of the New Testament, when a person becomes a follower of Christ,

[6] www.bbc.co.uk/news/world-31481797 (accessed 27 July 2023).

they have to die. They are called to carry their cross. It's not that they have to die physically, but they relinquish ownership of their life to God. His will becomes their will. His hopes become their hopes. His plans become their plans. His desires become their desires. It's not that their personality dies, or their sense of humour dies, or even their passion for life dies. It's just that their life is no longer their own (1 Corinthians 6:19-20). Their life is formed by the cross that they carry.

This cruciform life calls us to 'die daily' (1 Corinthians 15:31, NKJV). Every day I make a decision to crucify my will and be open to the Father's will. Each day I crucify my self-sins and let them die: self-exaltation, self-absorption, self-centredness. Each day I reject the comfortable compromise of conditional discipleship that says, 'I'll follow You, Jesus, but only if the cost isn't too great.' Every day I make a choice to climb back on the altar and offer myself to God all over again.

And while this all sounds like doom and gloom, it's actually the pathway to life. As always, the writers of the Bible tend to put things back to front. Jesus dies, and then He lives. The Christian dies, and then they live. It's our death that opens a door for life to come in. As we allow our lives to be shaped by the cross, we experience this 'hidden' life 'with Christ in God' (Colossians 3:3).

This hidden life creates in us an inner peace. It forms in us a security that cannot be shaken. It quietens the voice of the accuser, the devil, and it reminds us that we're never alone. It is a life 'invisible to spectators' (Colossians 3:3, *The Message*) but very real nonetheless.

One of the joys of being a local church pastor in the same location for a few decades is that you get to see people transition from one generation to another as their stage of life changes. Many times over the years I've sat with senior members of our congregation who, because of retirement, no longer have a role or a title. As time moves on, their bodies start to fail them, and they carry the grief of seeing friends and family pass away. But despite all those losses, they still have the most important thing of all: a hidden life with Christ.

You can take away their titles, but it doesn't affect their life with Christ. You can significantly reduce their income, but it doesn't affect their life with Christ. You can even take away their health, but this hidden, vibrant life that they have with Christ remains as strong and secure as it ever was.

Let me write this as sensitively as I can. If you're not experiencing this hidden life, could it be that you haven't died yet? If you are wondering why you aren't living, can I ask you if you've done any dying? Because to live deeply is to live a cruciform life. It is to loosen the grip on your life and to place it into the Father's hands.

Can God be trusted?

Of course, this invitation to relinquish our will, crucify the self and place our lives into the hands of God is all well and good, but it does raise an important question. Can God be trusted?

One of the things I loved to do when my children were a lot smaller than they are today was to throw them in the air and catch them. I guess many parents have done something similar. My children would smile and laugh, and even ask me to do it again when I stopped. I used to wonder why they loved it so much because, when you think about it, it's a fairly risky thing to do! And then it dawned on me: the reason they loved it so much was because they had never been dropped. It never once went through their minds that I wouldn't catch them because I had a 100 per cent success rate.

As time progresses, something happens to us. We grow up, and we get dropped. Someone promises to catch us, and they drop us. Someone guarantees never to leave us, but they leave. So we become cynical, sceptical and untrusting. We secretly decide that the only person we will ever trust is the person we see in the mirror. Me.

To then trust God becomes a big step for us to take. To 'trust in the LORD with all your heart and lean not on your own understanding' (Proverbs 3:5) becomes a considerable hurdle to jump over, especially when we've made a vow to only trust ourselves and no one else. In fact, I've discovered that what I fear the most reveals where I trust God the least.

A life of trusting God is built on a concrete belief that He is good. We can believe that He is all-powerful and all-knowing, but those attributes don't mean that He is good. God could be very strong, while also very bad. And so, to pray prayers of relinquishment, entrusting outcomes to God, requires us to be convinced that He is good.

When Jesus surrendered His will to the Father's will in Gethsemane, He did so knowing that for all eternity His Father had been loving and good. Even though Jesus was facing an unthinkable situation, He was convinced of His Father's goodness because He had known it and experienced it before. His trust was a response to known goodness.

Whenever I teach about spiritual formation, I encourage people to adopt the practice of journalling. For the uninitiated, a journal is a bit like a diary where you keep a record of God's activity in your life. You might write in it every day, once a week or once a month. There are no rules, and you don't get into heaven because you kept a journal; it's just helpful!

Why is it helpful? Because when there's trouble or trials, you can look back over the record you have kept of God's provision, protection, kindness and love, and it gives you the confidence to trust Him when the circumstances you are facing are painful or confusing. It's very difficult to trust in His goodness when everything in your life seems to be going wrong, if you haven't identified and enjoyed His goodness when everything is going right.

As Jesus faces the horror of the cross, He doesn't pretend that the pain isn't real. He asks for the 'cup' to be taken from Him (Matthew 26:39) because He knows that the suffering will be great. But in an act of sublime surrender, He trusts in the goodness of His Father because He's seen and experienced His Father's goodness for the whole of eternity.

The prayer of release

As this chapter comes to a conclusion, allow me to direct you towards another form of prayer that takes us from the shallows and into these deeper waters where we're now starting to swim. We may call it 'the prayer of release'; others might call it 'the practice of detachment'. It is to take the words of Jesus on the cross, 'Father, into your hands I commit my spirit' (Luke 23:46), and make them our own.

This detachment takes the shape of losing our lives so that we might find them (Mark 8:35).

It is to surrender all possessiveness and self-will in order to embrace the Father's will. It is to empty ourselves of control and invite the Spirit to fill us and to take control. It is to set goals and direction for our lives, but to leave the outcomes to God without us attempting to manipulate them or predict what they may be. It is to relinquish our lives so that we may truly live.

And so I take the words of Jesus, and they become my prayer of release.

> Into your hands I commit my need to be needed.
> Into your hands I commit my need to be noticed.
> Into your hands I commit my need to have it all together.
> Into your hands I commit my need to be successful.
> Into your hands I commit my need to be admired and accepted.
> Into your hands I commit my need to be in control.
> Into your hands I commit my life...
> ... and receive Your life in return.

> *Heavenly Father, teach me to trust You when I'm struggling to let go. Forgive my tendency to be a control freak, and help me to leave outcomes to You. Grant me the peace to follow You into the*

unknown, into the deeper waters, knowing that
You'll meet me and hold me there. Amen.

For reflection/discussion

- Take an overview of your life at present. Where is it that your grip is currently the tightest, and you are trying to control the outcomes?

- What would it look like for you to live a surrendered life and pray a prayer of relinquishment?

- If you are going to truly live, first you need to die daily. What would that mean for you?

- Reflect on this statement: 'What I fear the most reveals where I trust God the least.' Is this true for you, and if so, in what ways?

8

The Most Excellent Way

There are some spiritual rhythms that are to be practised daily, others weekly and some annually. At the end of every year, I have the habit of pulling out my journal and doing two things. First, I look back over the previous twelve months and assess whether or not I have achieved the goals I set at the start of the year. And second, I set goals for the year that lies ahead. My goals are usually focused on the number of miles I want to run, the amount of books I plan to read, some targets for my work life and a few ambitions for what I want to do with my family. After a few years, this practice became more of an academic exercise than a spiritual one, until one year I actually prayed about it.

Radical, I know.

On 31st December I paused and listened carefully to what God might say about the year ahead. In the stillness I realised that His goals for my life were very different from mine, and they were centred around my capacity to love. In those moments of prayer, as I asked the Lord what I should prioritise in the following twelve months, I woke up to the reality that the measure God uses to assess my success is love. Before He asks, 'Have you led well?', He asks, 'Have you loved well?' because He knows that I can't lead what I don't love (at least, not very well!). And so, with a blank page of my journal open in front of me, I sensed His probing question: 'Duncan, has your ability to love grown over this past year, and will it increase in the year that lies ahead?'

So often we gauge our success by worldly standards. We measure our career advancement, the size of our bank balance, the growth of our influence or reputation and the amount of material things we're amassing. These become the metrics by which we measure our lives. And for those of us who take our faith seriously, we may even measure our spiritual progress. The ability to prophesy. The level of our faith and our experience of miracles. Our giving to the poor. The kinds of things that the apostle Paul lists in 1 Corinthians 13 which, of course, he reminds us are worthless without love.

Your life is measured by your love.

Every time I come to God in prayer and ask Him for some direction, He annoyingly redirects me to love. 'Who have I placed in your life to love?' He asks. 'Are there attitudes in you that are contrary to love?' He enquires. 'Are you receiving love, so that you can give it away?' His questions continue.

As I was approaching a ministry milestone, my twenty-fifth wedding anniversary and my fiftieth birthday, I was asking God what He would want me to do with my life as I approached a new season. I was asking for discernment and direction. In that period of prayer, He whispered a simple word into my heart: 'I want you to do what love demands.' I was secretly hoping for something more strategic or dramatic than that, until I reminded myself that love must be my primary motivator, love must be my defining characteristic, and that without love I am nothing and I have nothing (1 Corinthians 13:2). Love is the measure of my depth. It is the measure of my life.

The disciple Jesus loved

The apostle John is an interesting character. In his Gospel, on five occasions he describes himself as 'the disciple whom Jesus loved' (John 13:23; 19:26; 20:2; 21:7; 21:20). He does that strange thing that some people do where they refer to themselves in the third person but everyone knows who they are talking about! Maybe John did it as an act of humility, not wanting to draw attention to himself. Maybe he did it as an act of pride, because he saw himself as uniquely special to Jesus. We don't know. All we know is that John had such a deep encounter with the loving presence of Jesus that it formed his identity and impacted everything he wrote about from that point onwards.

In the first of John's New Testament letters, he frequently calls us to live a life of love, but he does so knowing that we can only truly love others when we've encountered the love of God and have embraced the truth that we are loved.

John puts it this way: 'We love because he first loved us' (1 John 4:19).

Our quest to live deeply culminates in this life of love that John draws us into. It's a life where we lay our lives down for others in acts of caring and kindness, hospitality and service, friendship and compassion. This kind of life has its starting point in the Father's love. His love pours into our lives, then flows out of our lives. That's the motivation behind this beautiful verse that we all should store away in our memory banks:

> See what great love the Father has lavished on us, that we should be called children of God! And that is what we are!
> (1 John 3:1)

I love this verse for two reasons. First, because of John's excessive use of exclamation marks. I do that all that time. Whether I'm writing a message or an email, I find the best way to express my excitement about what I'm writing is to add an exclamation mark. Like John, I end up doing it at the end of every sentence! (There I go again!)

And second, I'm intrigued by John's use of the word 'see', because love is often something that we *feel*, not something that we *see*. So how do we *see* love?

On one level, some *see* God's love in the visible and tangible good gifts that He gives to us. In the same way that I demonstrate love for my wife by buying her another handbag, so God's love is made visible in the material, financial and relational gifts He gives to us freely.

But on another level, I think John is revealing something more significant here. He is teaching us that we *see* the Father's love when we look at Jesus. When we *see* the cross. When we *see* the way that Jesus lived a sacrificial life for others. In fact, Jesus said of Himself, 'Anyone who has seen me has seen the Father' (John 14:9). God has a disposition towards us, and it's seen in the life of Jesus.

God is not a sadistic monster who hates sinners and dangles them over the fiery pit of hell. No! We are prodigals (Luke 15:11-32) who have fallen into the hands of a loving Father, and His love is revealed when we *see* His Son.

The principle of reflection

You can only give something away that you have first received. You can't give money if you haven't received money. You can't give knowledge if you haven't first received knowledge. And you can't give love until you have received love. You get the idea!

I would describe this concept as 'the principle of reflection'.

It's something that is easily observed in the life of a child as they reflect or mirror whatever is directed towards them. You may have seen one of those short videos on social media where a parent pulls a funny face by sticking out their tongue, and their baby mirrors it straight back at them. More seriously, if a child experiences a lot of anger towards them, it's likely they will reflect that anger back into the world.

This principle of reflection is not restricted to children. Many adults take the hatred, unforgiveness, injustice and envy that is directed towards them, and they reflect it back into their communities. I would imagine that many of us have received an angry email or message, and we've fired one straight back. None of us is immune from that stuff.

There is, however, a positive side to this principle. We receive the Father's love that He has 'lavished on us', and then we reflect it into our families, our workplaces and our communities. You can't reflect that kind of love by studying it. You have to experience it. As you behold your Father's love and see that love revealed in Jesus, your heart is filled and it creates an overflow back into the world.

I know that some of you long for this kind of love. Those who should have loved you, didn't. Those who could have loved you, didn't. You were left at the hospital. You were left at the altar. You were left with a broken heart. You were left with the question, 'Does anyone love me?' And it's you I would encourage to 'see the Father's love'. His love, if you will allow it, will fill your heart with enough left over to give away. Enough for you to live loved.

Hearing the Father's voice

At the commencement of Jesus' ministry, and in an act of surrender and humility, He joins the queue to be baptised by John. At that moment the heavens are opened and Jesus hears the voice of His Father spoken over Him: 'You are my Son, whom I love; with you I am well pleased' (Luke 3:22).

I would like to suggest that those thirteen words spoken by the Father over His Son took such a deep root in Jesus' heart that they formed His identity, they confirmed His significance, and they filled His interior world with so much love that it spilled out wherever He went over the following three years.

Luke's Gospel tells us that straight after His baptism, Jesus goes toe to toe with the devil in the wilderness for forty intense days. On three occasions the devil comes to Jesus and taunts Him: 'Prove Yourself. Prove who You are. Do something spectacular.' And on each occasion Jesus resists, effectively saying, 'I don't need to demonstrate My worth because I heard a voice at the Jordan, and that voice told Me that I am loved and that I have nothing to prove.'

From that moment on, you can turn page after page of the Gospels and you can read how Jesus healed bodies and broken hearts; how He reached out in compassion to society's rejects and outcasts. And all these things He did as an overflow from a heart that was incredibly secure and full of the Father's love.

I believe that the deeper life is accessible to anyone who is able to claim as their core truth that they are a loved child of their heavenly Father. To live deeply is to hear the Father's voice speaking words of love over us. The trouble is, it's not always easy to hear His voice. We live in a world where there are many voices screaming at us: 'You're no good. You're ugly. You're worthless. You don't fit in.' It becomes very difficult to discern the Father's voice.

I live in a family that also struggles to hear their father's voice. As I said above, Helen and I have four children, and like most children today, they have headphones that are permanently attached to their ears, and it would take a substantial surgical procedure to remove them. It is therefore challenging for my children to hear their father's voice. If I shout at the top of my voice, asking someone to unload the dishwasher, no one hears their father's voice. If I call for someone to take out the rubbish bins, no one hears their father's voice. I do, however, find a miracle occurs when I whisper, 'Does anyone want a £10 note?' At that exact moment the deaf are healed, the father's voice is heard, and the previously lame children run as fast as they can towards their father's wallet!

While I'm trying to make you smile, there's a serious side to this. We live in a world of noise and a culture of many voices, and the noise and the voices tend to drown out the most important voice of all, the voice of our heavenly Father, the voice that tells us we are loved.

I would go as far as to say that some of us have become so accustomed to hearing those other voices that we have grown to trust them – those voices that tell us that we are unlovable and unlovely. We believe those lies as if they are truth, and as a result we run hard after success, popularity and power in an attempt to convince ourselves of our worth, of our belovedness. The trouble is, people and careers and organisations and material possessions let us down. And at that point we are left wondering if we have any value or worth at all. 'Am I really loved?' we ask.

If there's only one thing that you take away from this book, I would want it to be this: right now your heavenly Father is repeatedly whispering these words of love over you: 'You are my child, whom I love; with you I am well pleased.'

He has those words on repeat.

If you allow your Father's voice to be the primary voice that you tune into, if you allow His love to take a deep root in your heart, it will overflow into every area of your life. It will affect the way you approach your career, the way you think about money and the way you feel about yourself. It will change how you feel when someone else gets a promotion and you don't. It will change how you handle criticism and opposition. Because instead of seeing the whole of life as a competition where you have to out-perform everyone you know, you can rest in the reality that you are loved; that you are a loved child of your heavenly Father, that He is pleased with you and that He delights in you. You can enjoy being you when you enjoy being His.

Live like Jesus

Our four children are separated by twelve years, which meant that for eighteen consecutive years, Helen and I took at least one of our children to the same primary school, a couple of miles from our home. Now that season is over, I've noticed that taking a child to senior school is a very different process. They just jump out of the car and run. At primary school it was nothing like that. Along with other parents, Helen and I would stand with our children until the school gates were opened, and in that moment something would always happen that warmed my heart and gave me some hope for humanity. The parents of the youngest children would start hugging and kissing their children. You could hear many of them saying, 'Love you!' before sending them into the school day. Again, something you don't witness at the senior school gate!

I often wonder what that hug, kiss and 'Love you!' does for those children who receive it. Does it make them a daughter or son of that parent? No. Whether or not they get a hug and kiss, they still remain a daughter or a son. Does a child who doesn't hear a 'Love you!' doubt that they are a daughter or a son? No, I don't think so. They can still intellectually figure out that they are a daughter or a son of that parent.

So what does it do? What does the hug, kiss and 'Love you!' actually do for the child? I wonder if it does something in the heart. I believe it does something deep inside. I think it places a value and worth into the heart of the child. It helps them feel secure. And, if repeated multiple times, the child will grow up knowing that they are loved, and they are then equipped to live a life of love.

The apostle John's observation, 'in this world we are like Jesus' (1 John 4:17), becomes a reality for us once we have received the Father's love. We live like Jesus because we've heard the same voice that Jesus heard and we've received the same love that Jesus received. Without hearing that voice and receiving that love, our faith becomes legalistic and our actions driven by a need to perform. But when our hearts are full, our lives are moved and motivated by love.

How are you getting on with that?

I appreciate that when we discuss the theme of love it can sound a bit 'out there somewhere'. A bit intangible. For many people, 'love' describes that gooey feeling they get when they walk through glowing moonlight with someone they are close to. They get a shiver down their spine, and they call it love. For others, the word 'love' is used so casually it's almost lost its depth of meaning. We talk about loving cars, loving fast food and loving certain holiday destinations. Love can be equated with being nice, polite and friendly. This all seems wholly inadequate.

For the apostle Paul, there was no ambiguity when it came to his understanding and experience of love. For Paul, love wasn't a vague or nebulous concept. He was certain that we would be able to recognise it when we saw it.

For Paul, people who love will be growing in patience. There will be an increase in their kindness quota. The person who loves will never be envious of others, but will be thankful for everything they have been given. They will treat people who are different from them with the greatest respect. Their love will be evidenced in their rejection of pride and their willingness to take the path of humility. Rather than having a short fuse of anger, they will be people of peace. The person who loves will be quick to forgive, they will protect others, they will always maintain hope and they will never give up on someone because their love 'always perseveres' (see 1 Corinthians 13:4-7).

Paul was clear that this is what an overflow of love looks like. That's how we measure love. That's the scorecard. He calls it 'the most excellent way' (1 Corinthians 12:31b). It's the path that Jesus took, and with a heart full of the Father's love, it's the path you are invited to tread with Him too.

> *Heavenly Father, I long to hear Your voice telling me that I'm loved. Help me to hear it clearly so that I'll never doubt that it's true. I want to love other people in the way You love me, reflecting Your tender kindness to all people that I meet. May love be the overflow from my life. Amen.*

For reflection/discussion

- How might God's goals be different from the goals you currently have for your life?

- If your life is measured by your love, how are you doing?

- Reflect on these three questions: 'Who has God placed in your life to love?', 'Are there attitudes in you that are contrary to love?', 'Are you receiving love, so that you can give it away?' What are the answers you come up with?

- Why do you think these words from your heavenly Father are the most important words you can ever hear? 'You are my child, whom I love; with you I am well pleased.'

Epilogue

Many times, I've sat in the comfort of my deckchair, enjoying the warmth of the sun on my skin and the feel of the sand on my toes, and I've shouted to my kids who are enjoying the unpredictable waves of the sea, 'Don't go too deep!'

As a cautious and caring parent, I want to keep my children safe, and so I urge them to avoid experiencing the deep waters. I'm more relaxed when they paddle in the shallows, rather than when their courageous spirits kick in and they get an adrenaline rush from swimming into the depths where their feet can longer touch the ground.

There's safety in the shallow water.

But from the safety of the shallows, every child looks out into the deep and wonders what's out there.

As they stand in the shallow water, they say to themselves, 'There must be more than this.' They stare, longingly, at the deep waters, believing that there's an adventure waiting out there for them. It feels risky to take their feet off the bottom and swim away from the shore, but somewhere inside they know that this is where the adventure begins. So they go deeper.

That's been the cry of this book: to leave the shallows and go deeper. As an act of rebellion against the superficial, consumerist form of Christianity that calls us to follow Jesus so that we become healthy and wealthy, we've been called into deeper waters. It's a costly call. It's often the way of surrender and sacrifice. It feels just a bit risky.

To *live deeply* requires us to stay close to Jesus. To sit in the stillness of His presence when the culture promotes lifestyles of hurried distraction; to put down unseen roots in an age of mobility, that will aid our resilience in tough times; to prioritise prayer, seeing and seeking God in the ordinary; to embrace mystery, even when we're craving for certainty.

To *live deeply* requires us to live like Jesus; to choose humility when the culture is centred on self-promotion; to feel our emotions, because they reveal the passions God has hidden in our hearts; to let go of our need to control outcomes, and to offer up prayers of relinquishment; to desire love, because that is the 'most excellent way'.

From the shallows we cry, 'There must be more than this.'

And so we pray, 'Jesus, take us deeper.'

Also by Duncan Clark:

How are you living your life? Are you half-hearted or *Wholehearted*?

In this dynamic and accessible book, Duncan Clark casts an inspirational vision of what life is like when we fully commit to God and all He has for the one life we have been given. Using the Old Testament story of Caleb as a foundation, we learn what it looks like to live a life wholly devoted to God.

Insightful questions and a 'Habits for the heart' guide make this a perfect book to read with other people who also know that the transformation of their lives starts with the reshaping of their hearts. Follow in the footsteps of Caleb and be *Wholehearted* for God!

Praise for *Wholehearted*:

'"Above all else, guard your heart" (Proverbs 4:23) – but just how do we do this? *Wholehearted* answers this question, and it does so with beautiful clarity, accessibility and insight.'
Mark Pugh, Lead Pastor, Rediscover Church, Exeter

'An inspiring and challenging read. Duncan has captured so beautifully what it means to be completely sold out to the Lord in this day and age.'
James Aladiran, Founder And Director, Prayer Storm